THE
WEB 2.0
JOB
FINDER

Funded by
MISSION COLLEGE
Carl D. Perkins Vocational and Technical Education Act Grant

WINNING SOCIAL MEDIA STRATEGIES TO GET THE JOB YOU WANT FROM FORTUNE 500 HIRING PROS

THE
WEB 2.0
JOB
FINDER

BRENDA GREENE AND COLEEN BYRNE

CAREER PRESS

THE WEB 2.0 JOB FINDER
EDITED AND TYPESET BY KATHRYN HENCHES
Cover design by Howard Grossman/12E Design
Printed in the U.S.A.

To order this title, please call toll-free 1-800-CAREER-1 (NJ and Canada: 201-848-0310) to order using VISA or MasterCard, or for further information on books from Career Press.

CAREER PRESS

The Career Press, Inc.
220 West Parkway, Unit 12
Pompton Plains, NJ 07444
www.careerpress.com

Library of Congress Cataloging-in-Publication Data

Greene, Brenda.
        The Web 2.0 job finder : winning strategies to get the job you want from
fortune 500 hiring pros / by Brenda Greene and
        Coleen Byrne.
                p. cm.
        Includes bibliographical references and index.
        ISBN 978-1-60163-158-9 – ISBN 978-1-60163-668-3 (ebook) 1. Job hunting
2. Online social networks. 3. Web 2.0. I.
        Byrne, Coleen. II. Title.

        HF5382.7.G727 2011
        650.140285'6754—dc22

                                                        2011003530

Dedication

*To my first social network, brothers and sisters, Terry
Byrne, Mary D'Annibale, Doreen Murray, Patty Leonard,
Alice Good, Myles Byrne*
—Brenda

To the jobs I have worked the hardest at, searched the longest for, and loved the most: daughter, wife, mother
—Coleen

~ ~ ~

In Memory
Chris Nutile
December 21, 1967 to January 2, 2011
http://1000memories.com/christopher-nutile

*Contributor, connector, industry leader, a friend,
and forever a part of our social network.*

*Chris was actively involved in raising donations for Kiva.org,
his favorite charity. Please help us continue his passion for
Kiva and join his team: www.kiva.org/team/cnutile_legacy*

~ ~ ~

Acknowledgments

Lisa Beauclaire, PHR, specialist, HR Sourcing and Diversity, American Family Insurance; Shelley Bird, executive vice president, Public Affairs, Cardinal Health; Karen Bradbury, assistant vice president, Talent Management Strategies, Unum; Laurie Byrne, vice president, Global Staffing and Talent Development, Stryker Corporation; Martin Cepeda,* senior university recruiter, Human Resources; Ian Decker, director, Corporate Recruiting, MetLife; Megan Dick, PHR, manager, Human Resources, Cameron; Charlotte Frank, PhD, senior vice president, Research and Development, The McGraw-Hill Companies; Jim Gattuso, director, Staffing and Recruitment, CSC; Charles Greene,** vice president, Trading Systems Development, NYSE Euronext; Ron Gosdeck, vice president, Recruitment, Unisys; Kathy Hooson, recruiter, Staffing, Hewlett-Packard; Kirk Imhof, group director, Recruiting, Ryder System, Inc.; Brian Jensen, vice president, Talent Acquisition, The McGraw-Hill Companies; Eric E. Kaulfuss, director, Talent, CIGNA; Laura Terenzi Khaleel, director, Talent Acquisition Strategies, Pitney Bowes; Matthew Lavery, manager, Corporate Workforce Planning, UPS; Paul Marchand, vice president, Global Talent Acquisition, PepsiCo; Debbie Mathew, strategic business partner, Human Resources, Hewlett-Packard;

Heather McBride-Morse,* SPHR/GPHR, manager, Human Resources; Keith McIlvaine,*** global social media recruitment lead, Global Recruiting Operations, Unisys; Dan McMackin, manager, Public Relations, UPS; David McMichael, assistant vice president and manager, Staffing Strategies and Programs, SAIC; Cindy Nicola,*** vice president, Global Talent Acquisition, Electronic Arts; Shannon Pelissero, zone manager, Human Resources, PPG Industries; Michael Peltyn, vice president, Human Resources, ARIA – CityCenter, MGM Resorts International; Claudia M. Reilly, national program manager, Recruitment, Avnet, Inc.; Carolyn Rice,*** director, Talent Management, North and South America, Kellogg's; Mike Rickheim, vice president, Global Talent Acquisition, Newell Rubbermaid; Sean Splaine, leadership recruiter, Human Resources, Google, Inc.; Vincent Taguiped,* manager, Recruitment; Scott R. Taylor, partner, McDonald's; Stan Weeks, senior recruiting manager/program manager, College Relations, Weyerhaeuser; Abigail Whiffen, director, Global Recruiting Operations, Unisys; Lisa Whittington, vice president, Human Resources, Host Hotels & Resorts.

In addition to the Fortune 500 professionals, we tapped into the expertise of Lissa Freed,*** vice president, Human Resources, Activision; Brett Goodman, recruiter, EdisonLearning, Inc.; Chris Nutile, director, MediaLink Executive Search, a division of MediaLink, LLC; Mike Troiano, principal, Holland-Mark; Shally Steckerl, executive vice president, Arbita; Erik Qualman, author of Socialnomics; Helen Cunningham, director of communications, DTCC; Ken Nussbaum, CPA and consultant, K. Nussbaum & Associates; Olga O'Donnell, monetization strategist, MSN; Paula Cuneo; Rich Sanchez; Diana Donovan, marketing director, LifeStreet Corporation; Amy Mehta, account executive, AOL.

Thank you also to individuals in the communication and public relations departments of Fortune 500 companies who arranged some of the telephone interviews. Some remained behind the scenes while others took a more active role, individuals such as J. Patrick Anderson, vice president, Corporate Affairs, Stryker Corporation; Carol Wallace, director, External Com-munications, Pitney Bowes; Laura Luke, vice president, Media Relations, SAIC; Jim Kerr, vice president, Global Public Relations and Regional Communications, Unisys;

Gloria Barone-Rosario, APR, Corporate Communications, CIGNA; David Murphy, vice president, Human Resources, McGraw-Hill; Cindy Haas, director, Corporate Communications, Ryder System, Inc.; Emily Phillips, specialist, Public Relations, MetLife; Michelle Gorel, vice president, Public Relations, Avnet, Inc.; Connie Bryant, manager, Public Relations, Newell Rubbermaid; Chris Grandis, director, Public Relations, CSC; Jim Sabourin, vice president, Corporate Communications, Unum.

To people within our social network who opened their networks to us for this project or have in the past: Dave Dickman, Tracee Nalewak, Amy Smith, Kathleen Haley, Kym Nelson, Tabitha Hayes, Neal Wilson, Heather Peterson, Lisa Greenberg, Susan Hahn, Dan Gallagher, Keith Nyhouse, Clara Kym, Mike Janover, Lucinda Mac-Donell, Robin Boyar, Marc Cote, Patricia Neuray, Carrie Tice, Evan Rudowski, Patrick Toland, Ken Rutkowski, Jill Robinson, Kim Bennett, EJ Vongher, Joni Cooper, Ken Phipps, Karen Rose, Ronnie Planalp, Kari Allen, Kristin Motta, Caitlin Pulleyblank, Torrey Lincoln, Rick Vorhaus, Joni Cooper, Carol Terakawa, Leigh Reichley, Robert Leonard.

We are also grateful to our friends and families for their support and encouragement: Myles Greene, Rose Anna Greene, Marie Greene, Rob Scala, Lorna Milbauer, Kathy Murphy, Suzann Anderson, Myra Williamson, Sabina Horton, Sheila Nadata, Mary Lou Anelante, Sharon Guadagno, Angelo Guadagno, Ryan Wener, Myles Wener, Liam Wener, Megan Byrne, Susan Guadagno, Lynne Hale, friends at Naturally Yoga, and friends at the Sunday Night.

Finally, we would like to thank our collaborators: Joelle Delbourgo, from Joelle Delbourgo Associates; Jacquie Flynn, our agent from Joelle Delbourgo Associates, who nudged us toward the job market and offered her own insight on social media; our editorial and production contacts at Career Press, Michael Pye, Kirsten Dalley, Gina Hoogerhyde, Kate Henches, Jeff Piasky.

*   Some Fortune 500 individuals requested we not name their companies.
**   Recently retired from NYSE Euronext.
***   Recently moved to another position at a different company.

Contents

A note about quoted material in this book...

Unless otherwise indicated in the text, all quotations were derived from interviews conducted in the time period from 2007 to 2010. All such quotations are completely original to this book, and appear with express permission of the persons interviewed.

Introduction

Any one of us who has looked for a job during our careers
knows that networking has been, still is, and will always be
the best way to find a position. So now we have technology
working in our favor to allow us and enable us to network
more broadly and more quickly—in real time.
—Laura Terenzi Khaleel
Director, Talent Acquisition Strategies
Pitney Bowes

Some things never change—and some things never stop
changing. In recent years, the hiring process has fallen into
the second category. Back in 2004, I wrote *Get the Interview
Every Time,* about how the digital world was turning the
job market upside down. I based the book on the input I
received from 50 Fortune 500 hiring professionals. A few
years later, because so many job seekers were still clinging
to the ubiquitous hard-copy resume printed on expensive
stationery and blindly mailed to a batch of varied employers, I subsequently wrote two more books urging readers to
go electronic. Targeted keyword search became the back-
bone of the new electronic hiring process and job seekers
needed to align their job searches with those who were doing the hiring.

Now, just as we all got comfortable again (or as comfortable as you can get in a job market with nearly 10 percent unemployment), along comes social media—Twitter, Facebook, LinkedIn, MySpace, and YouTube, to name a few. What do these social networking sites have to do with the job market?

Pretty much the same thing that they have to do with your social life. Whether you have weak ties or strong ties, using social networks can make your connections grow more robust, extend your reach, help you maintain relationships with people who historically you would have lost touch with, and enable you to target employers with laser focus. Essentially, social network sites provide rich databases that allow you to easily manage your connections with a personal touch—photos, videos, snippets of what's happening in your life— while keeping a keen eye on your profession. Provided you participate regularly, your circle of friends and associates can expand exponentially. Social media allows networking—one of the most essential components of the job search—to unfold almost effortlessly.

Think of it this way. Remember all those coworkers from your last job at XYZ Company—the ones you worked with for 40 hours a week for five years, or the ones you went to lunch with at the neighborhood deli two or three times a week, or the ones you played softball with at the annual company picnic? Before social networking, you probably lost touch with all but one or two of them because you didn't have the time or wherewithal to keep track of everybody.

That's all changed now that social media has gained a foothold. With relative ease, you can "link" with most of the people you worked with in the accounting department of your former employer, or you can share your Facebook page with the guys in your fraternity or sisters in your sorority, or you can post updates for your friends, classmates, and associates who are following your tweets on Twitter, or form a closer tie with an alumnus from your college. Through the ease of electronic communication—whether it is sending e-mail, viewing photos, posting brief status updates on daily life, or making comments in forums or even blogs—you can stay actively connected to a wider network. People who in years gone by would have fallen by the wayside as lost connections can now become part of a dynamic and engaged network.

In an age of economic disruption, it makes perfect sense to position yourself to take advantage of new opportunities. Retooling and rebuilding are real possibilities—and not just for companies. The job market has been merciless and you need to be able to respond quickly—before your job is gone. Tapping into your connections when you are out of work is too little, too late. As Carolyn Rice, director of Talent Management for Kellogg's, said, "It's so much more important to do this when you have a job than when you are desperately looking for a new one."[1] You need to identify people in your network who are important to your business. Especially in the event that you do need a job, those relationships need to be thriving. Social networking allows those relationships to stay current, so you can grab a cup of coffee with a coworker, shoot an occasional note to check in, talk about the latest happenings at a company you are targeting, and send congrats on work promotions or company changes.

It's about the brand

Virtual connections are quickly becoming the networking tool of choice, and work is the new hot topic of conversation. This development did not escape the notice of America's largest and most successful employers, who saw the need to engage on social networks, too. Claudia Reilly, the national program manager of Recruitment at Avnet, Inc., said, "The new media has changed hiring dramatically. Even from the beginning when applicants began applying online—maybe starting heavily five to seven years ago where that became the mode of application—to now, the volume of applicants you get through the different venues, such as blogs and everything out there, has changed the entire process. And it also has had an impact on how we view and look at resumes."[2]

While Fortune 500 companies create their own online communities—sites where they not only extol their brand but also cast their nets for new employees—job seekers, too, are developing an online brand. What is personal branding in the age of social networking? Not to oversimplify, but it is the sum total of everything you say online. That's your brand. And according to the Fortune 500 professionals we spoke to, it's a good idea to be as judicious about what you publicly announce online as these billion-dollar companies are about their brands.

Social networks growing up

When social networks began, they were youthful domains where teenagers and college-age students worked out their angst, determined the pecking order or just hung out chatting with friends—without restraint or seeming purpose. But eventually, especially with the introduction of the business network, LinkedIn, in 2003, and the subsequent buy-in from the students' parents on Facebook, YouTube, and MySpace a few years later, the demographics of social networks began to age. Social networking started to grow up, and participants leveraged their time spent chatting and put it to good use by spotting career opportunities so that they could find a job before they actually needed a job.

David McMichael, an assistant vice president and manager of staffing strategies and programs at SAIC (Science Applications International Corporation), a Fortune 500 company that employs 45,000 people worldwide, said: "I think it's a common misconception that [social networks are for] a younger audience. In fact, through this whole process, you'll start to look at some of this demographic data and when you look at Twitter, the majority of people on there are between 30 and 45. Our target audience has a footprint on these sites."[3]

When the opportunity to write *The Web 2.0 Job Finder* presented itself, I was fairly new to social media. Actually, my kids would say I was stumbling around, making my share of blunders. They often reminded me how public the medium is, but every time I asked my youngest daughter to explain the ins-and-outs of Facebook or Twitter, she ran the other way, so I started doing my own research and began paying attention to those who were at home in social networking.

That's when I tapped into Coleen Byrne's expertise. Coleen has worked in the Internet industry since 1996 and was most recently sales director at Yahoo! In addition, she has worked for CNET, Excite, and IGN, and she has both international and domestic experience in Internet advertising sales and operations, Internet marketing, and Internet business development. Coleen's career has grown with the Internet industry, and it is tightly integrated into her daily life—both personally and professionally. She is also my niece and was one of my first contacts on Facebook. I followed her lead. A conversation about social networks began and her enthusiasm became contagious. We started talking to some experts.

Fortune 500 expertise and other insiders

As in four earlier books (one on business writing and three on the job market), *The Web 2.0 Job Finder* is based on the expertise of Fortune 500 professionals. Professionals from these companies have a deep knowledge of how trends play themselves out on a large scale. Fortune 500 companies are the largest and most successful business-es in America and their reach is extensive. UPS (United Parcel Ser-vice), one of the companies we sought for *The Web 2.0 Job Finder,* is the second-largest employer in the United States with a workforce of 400,000-plus. Dan McMackin, manager of Public Relations, and Matthew Lavery, manager of Corporate Workforce Planning, have been with UPS since the days of paper resumes. Having mastered Web 1.0 on a large scale for UPS, they knew instinctively that social networking was the next "evolution" in hiring. As Lavery said, "If we don't start building our process now, we are going to be left be-hind. We want to be sure that we keep growing and we understand how the community is going to work and be part of that community and grow with it."[4] The Fortune 500 employers who did agree to be interviewed for this book echoed Lavery's claim, but we should men-tion we reached out to more than 400 Fortune 500 companies, and many of them said they were too new to the game to offer any guid-ance on social networking. Without a doubt, social networking is still evolving, but the 35 Fortune 500 professionals we spoke to provide a significant benchmark.

Because the Web 2.0 job market is so dynamic, we thought it would be a good idea to tap into the expertise of smaller, cutting-edge companies as well. Small and midsize companies employ more than 65 percent of working Americans. By virtue of the fact that many of these employers are smaller than most Fortune 500 companies, they usually respond more quickly to new directions. These smaller companies often are "nimble" and open to innovation—especially as these developments trend toward protocol. As a result, their perspective on social media provides a true 360-degree view of what's happening in the 2.0 marketplace.

Finally, the picture *The Web 2.0 Job Finder* paints would not be complete unless we spoke to those individuals in the trenches of the job market—recruiters and job seekers discovering opportunities. You'll hear about their success stories—even in this squeezed economy—and how social media made the challenging process of finding a job more fruitful and definitely swifter.

Because our experts focused on LinkedIn, Facebook, Twitter, and YouTube, we did too. As far as the job market goes, you have to follow the big numbers in social media. Companies zero in on the sites with the most users, but, again, it's an ever-evolving medium. Five years from now, the Web may morph into 3.0 or 4.0 or 5.0 and it may be a completely different animal, so who needs to read this book now? We think *The Web 2.0 Job Finder* will help job seekers who want to turn social media into a powerful career tool; it will help those who want to understand how Fortune 500 companies are using it; and it will help those who need to revise their attitude and get their feet wet without creating havoc. The book is not a how-to on navigating specific social sites; there are plenty of in-depth books on those topics. Rather, *The Web 2.0 Job Finder* is a practical guide to understanding how social media is changing hiring—from a hiring professional's perspective—and how it is changing our lives in the process.

Cautionary tales

So much has been said about the pitfalls of social media—you are being watched, you are being judged—that it's become a favorite bogeyman. Even Eric Schmidt, CEO of Google, added his own warnings when he told a group of journalists at the *Wall Street Journal* that "...every young person one day will be entitled automatically to change his or her name on reaching adulthood in order to disown youthful hijinks stored on their friends' social media sites."[5] We don't want to scare anyone away from social media—it's a powerful tool when looking for a job—but we would be remiss if we didn't address the issue of privacy and the need for discretion. We encourage you to engage and interact on social platforms, but if you are new to social networking, remember that all your online conversations and musings are public. Pay particular attention to Chapter 4 if you are new to the game.

Even though we are fairly certain that by now everyone has digested all the dos and don'ts of social networking—with only the uninformed posting photos of Saturday night's beer bong party—you also need to practice online common sense. You can still do a lot of damage to your personal brand and disqualify yourself for a job with your online postings by allowing others to infer that you are a complainer, a slouch, a misanthrope, or just plain difficult.

Why network?

The key to networking is determining specifically what you want to do and then connecting with the people you know. If you can position yourself as a solution to a company's problem—and you can communicate this to your network—your contacts will usually want to help you in any way they can. But as Ian Decker, a director of Talent Acquisition at MetLife, said, "You need to come out of your shell and let people know that you are looking."[6] Social networking allows you to do this in a friendly, non-obligatory manner. It allows you to connect with your strong alliances—and your weak ones, too.

Most job seekers are aware that networking is by far the best tool for finding a job, but too many still approach the hunt in a hit-or-miss fashion. We want to emphasize in *The Web 2.0 Job Finder* that securing a good job that has staying power is rarely just a matter of luck. Focused research, a targeted resume, insight into the full hiring cycle, keyword search, skillbuilding and follow-up are all essential components of finding a good job. Although it may seem Web 1.0, we cover these traditional topics too because these facets of the job hunt are as relevant in the Web 2.0 world as they were 10, 20, 30 years ago. Social networking is not an antidote to a highly competitive job market; rather, it is a tool—a powerful tool when used appropriately, especially when it's used *before* you actually need a new job.

Not just any job

For the last few years, during the worst job market since the Great Depression, prospects have been limited and/or nonexistent. Nearly 15 million Americans are out of work. *The Web 2.0 Job Finder* will help you navigate your way through the "funnel," so you can zero in on the jobs that are a good match for your skills and qualifications. Finding and securing meaningful work is crucial, no matter what the economic climate is, but you need to be deliberate, focused, and aware of the new criteria. Research will play a big part in getting the type of meaningful work you deserve.

Exactly what *is* meaningful work? We like Malcolm Gladwell's definition. The author of *Outliers* said, "...autonomy, complexity, and a connection between effort and reward are, most people agree, the three qualities that work has to have if it is to be satisfying."[7] Engaging work that allows you to problem-solve while compensating you sufficiently is available—even in an ailing economy. You just need to know how to use your toolbox to discover it. *The Web 2.0 Job Finder* can help you. Our goal is to create a career book that answers the questions a job seeker may have regarding the 2.0 marketplace. Kellogg's talent director, Carolyn Rice, said her company fills a very high number of its open jobs through networking, so job seekers can significantly improve their chances of getting hired with a wide networking circle. With social networking, those weak ties that we all accumulate throughout a career can actually become some of your strongest allies.

We spend more time working—usually 40 hours or more a week—than doing anything else, and we all know that work has the potential to define and fulfill us or make us miserable. If you value your well-being, your health (physical and psychological), and financial prospects, then it's critical to find and secure a position that allows you to realize your potential. We agree with Sigmund Freud, who said, "The key to happiness is meaningful love and meaningful work." *The Web*

2.0 Job Finder will focus on your work, even though understanding social networking may indeed have broader applications.

SAIC's David McMichael said, "I'm hopeful that the book will help people come to the realization that [social media] is here to stay. I read recently that one in eight married couples met through social media. That's a pretty powerful statistic. It's harder to find a spouse than it is to find a job or people to fill it. Within the next 10 years, people will use social media to find an employer and the numbers could be staggering."[8]

Chapter 1

Working Your Brand

I have a hard time saying that personal and professional networks should be completely separate because I think, at the end of the day, to really be a good networker you figure out how to mesh those two things well.
—Mike Rickheim
Vice President of Global Talent Acquisition
Newell Rubbermaid

Who are you? You've probably been asking yourself that question your entire life—without ever coming to any conclusive answer. Even when life is at a standstill, some variable introduces itself and you are forced to reformulate and sometimes even reinvent yourself. That's the nature of life. You change, you grow, you accommodate the new—both the good and the bad. That's why the idea of personal branding may sound almost counterintuitive to you. The concept is too fixed, too stale, too conformist. You are a human being, after all, not a product or service. But let's look at it from another perspective. Even if you are fluid, elusive, and constantly changing, there's no denying that wherever you go you leave an impression.

That impression is the topic of this chapter. That impression is your personal brand.

Ten years ago, very few people referred to this impression as a personal brand. Instead, in your private life, it was often called your personality or maybe your essence. In your professional life, it was called your image. For the most part, it was fairly easy to develop these identities separately. Each facet that made you you could be neatly compartmentalized and tucked away until you chose to showcase yourself—whether it was at home, in the workplace, in the community, or with your friends. You had many faces, and not too many people got a glimpse of the all-inclusive you. Not to underestimate your value in any way, but most people, with the exception of your nearest and dearest, didn't think all the intimate particulars of your life were exactly relevant.

And you're not even in show biz

Fast-forward to the digital world of 2011, where information about you can be pulled from thin air and reassembled—inexpensively, quickly and easily—into a full-figured profile. Anyone who has done research on the Internet knows Google is a beautiful tool, but this fact doesn't always soothe the soul when those compartments that were carefully (or perhaps not so carefully) constructed burst wide open and all those online musings, inquiries, opinions, likes, and dislikes become transparent.

Exactly when did this happen? We are a talky bunch. No language has more words than the English language (more than a million according to the Global Language Monitor).[1] It is also the language of the Internet (maybe not officially, but in 2010 there were approximately 100 million more English users than Chinese users).[2] Language—actually usage—is a good indicator of what's important to us in our daily lives, and, according to the GLM, if a new word is cited at least 25,000 times, it's time to add it to the lexicon.

Just in case you're wondering what the official one-millionth word of the English language is...On Wednesday, June 10, 2009, the Global Language Monitor crowned **Web 2.0** as the one-millionth *word* (yes, *word*) in the English language.

What is Web 2.0?

So you understand why we chose to name the book *The Web 2.0 Job Finder*, a little history may help. At a conference in 2004, Tim O'Reilly, a leading advocate of open source,[3] said when the Dot-com bubble burst in 2001, the Internet reshuffled. The wheat separated from the chaff. The strong—Google, Craigslist, Yahoo!, and eBay, to name a few—survived, and the weak fell, at least temporarily.[4]

It took some time to recover from the 2001 fallout, but the next big thing (a phrase many were reluctant to utter after the bubble burst) began to sprout from the wheat...and the chaff. Software platforms developed that began to "harness the collective intelligence" of users (Digg, Wikipedia). These were platforms with rich layers of information marked by increasing interactivity. Essentially these platforms were enormous databases of information that cost nothing to use. To be successful, they had to be popular and engaging. In effect, the more people who jumped on board, the richer the data became.

For a few years, so many social media venues surfaced that it was difficult to decide where to participate. Some users created profiles in Plaxo while some ventured into LinkedIn, some stayed loyal to Friendster while others migrated to MySpace, some contributed to Digg while others engaged with Reddit, some tuned into YouTube while others proclaimed the virtues of Vimeo, and so on. The platforms managed to coexist peacefully—with each touting its own uniqueness—but eventually it was user popularity that determined value. Preferences began to make a difference. As Kirk Imhof, a group director at Ryder System, Inc., said, "The venue for social media is particularly good if it's used en masse—providing an employer access to many potential candidates. We have had our best success with social media sites that are used by many."[5]

The migration to certain platforms began. In 1995 you may have been able to find a long-lost school chum on Classmate.com, but, 10 years later, you could fully engage in conversations and share photos and videos with them on Friendster and MySpace. Soon LinkedIn (2003), Facebook (2004), YouTube (2005), and Twitter (2006) interrupted the conversations with their own slants. Blogs, microblogs, forums, comments—it seemed everybody had a lot to talk about.

Once these sites won their way into our hearts, the dialogue became enthusiastic, even reckless at times. User-generated content was the new game in town and social networking nudged itself into our daily lives. A frenzy of free speech ensued.

Marshall McLuhan, in 1964, said, "The medium is the message."[6] It's just as true today, so, with this in mind, what distinguishes the Web 2.0 medium from other forms of communication? We are going to let others go into greater depth on this topic, but for the purposes of *The Web 2.0 Job Finder,* we think social media is set apart from other communication tools by (1) its public, communal, interactive nature, (2) the minutiae of the conversation, and (3) the speed, extension, and economy of getting the message out. In many respects, social media is a perfect vehicle for a job search.

The 2.0 job market

This is a broad overview of Web 2.0, but because this book is about the job market, suffice it to say that social networking—regardless of the nonstop warnings against publicly airing private details—is quickly becoming the tool of choice for communicating and connecting with your colleagues. Keith McIlvaine, a former global social media recruitment lead at Unisys, said on Twitter, "Social networking is not new. Platform is new. Networking has been happening from dawn of time." (September 28, 2010.)[7]

It's true: Humans have always networked; survival often depended on it. Social connection is a constant; it's just the medium—the "platform"—that constantly changes. Although nothing has ever been more rewarding than a face-to-face, humans have continually enhanced the reach of communication with one medium after the other: mail, Pony Express, telegram, telephone, e-mail. We are good at connecting with others. That's what we do; we share information, so when connections grew digitally, the conversation organically seeped into different compartments of our lives. Hiring was one of them.

Knowing that networking is probably the best way to secure a new position, job seekers eagerly connected virtually with their colleagues—past and present. With social media they could keep in touch (and interact) with scores of associates—whether they were in the neighboring town or halfway across the globe. And it didn't take long before companies realized they too could cast a wider net over available applicants by engaging them through social media. Ryder's Kirk Imhof said, "We continue to look at best practices in recruiting and we continue to leverage the tools that our candidates are using—and their favorite hangouts are where we want to be."[8]

Statistics confirm that the best way to find a job is through networking.[9] While the exact numbers vary on exactly how many jobs are filled as a direct result of networking—and that could mean anything from "Hey Joe, I noticed ABC Company is hiring" to "Give me your resume, Joe, and I'll show our hiring manager"—a savvy job seeker knows it's essential to tap into his or her contacts when looking for a new opportunity. That means you need to pick up the telephone, send a former colleague an e-mail, attend an industry function—or even a family get-together—and start asking for direction and suggestions. Nowadays it also means tapping into your online social network.

What are you all about?

But back to the crux of the chapter: personal branding. Before the networking process begins, it's important to cultivate an online portrait of yourself that enhances your prospects. That means you will have to market your skills and attributes. That could mean anything from creating a full-bodied, professional LinkedIn profile to leveraging some of the damage on Facebook by adjusting your privacy settings so that your musings and photos are not as public. You need to start thinking about your personal brand before the dialogue about a career move even begins.

Ideally, you are still employed before you even start thinking about a new job. That's the best position to work from, and a strategy that allows you to make a thoughtful choice about where your career is headed, but not everyone is so lucky. We are still recuperating from the worst job loss since the Great Depression, so making a move in this economic climate can require a fair amount of clairvoyance, with only the most adventurous opting to change jobs when nearly 15 million people are unemployed. The good news is that the job market is bound to change. If a robust economy is not around the corner, there's a very good chance it's hovering around the bend. Regardless, whether you are actively looking or passively considering a new job, what better time than now to build your brand?

Take an in-depth look at your work self. Most of us spend more time working than doing anything else, so it's important to identify the activities that engage you fully and allow you to make a strong and unique contribution. Do you love research? Do you enjoy solving logistics issues? Do you meet your deadlines without having palpitations? Do you passionately enjoy generating new leads? Do you love the interaction with customers? Do you like to mentor those who have less experience? Do you have a knack for discovering the perfect code? Do you delegate without alienating? You get the picture. Whatever wakes you up or plugs you in when you are working is probably your strong point(s). It is also your personal brand and what makes you, you.

If your current work does not match your real strengths—and there are plenty of people who hold jobs that are not fulfilling—then there's another way to approach this issue. Brian Tracy, in *Eat That Frog,* says you should ask yourself, "Why are you on the payroll?"[10] You need to be crystal clear about this. Do you troubleshoot issues and offer an anticipated fix? Do you organize databases so that they are logical and efficient? Do you develop financial and marketing strategies for customers to increase sales and gross margins? Do you coordinate activities for all aspects of merchandising? Even if you are not particularly fond of the activities you spend eight hours a day doing, you must be good at them; otherwise you wouldn't be on the payroll. So, if your job doesn't match your strengths—ideally at least—think about the things you are good at and which of these transferable skills you plan to bring forward to your next position because these skills are going to be part of your brand also.

If you're thinking, "This is too much trouble. I just want to find a good job," then maybe you need to ask yourself exactly what a good job means. A case in point is Jeanne Smith. Back when business was booming (not so long ago actually), Jeanne was able to support herself by selling her paintings in galleries. She's an excellent artist, but the market dried up in the economic downturn. She needed to retool, so she enrolled in a certification program that would allow her to make a very good living while she painted in her free time. The new job was in the service field. There were plenty of open positions in this field, so Jeanne didn't have trouble finding a job, but she did have trouble *keeping* a job. The new work didn't suit her; in fact, it was totally alien to her. But, out of stubbornness and desperation, the newly certified Jeanne kept trying to put a square peg into a round hole. She took one service job after another, until her body told her (back trouble, Lyme's disease, migraine headaches) what her mind refused to accept: it wasn't a good fit.

Imagine another scenario for Jeanne. If she had identified her strengths (and they were obvious), she could have seen that her creative talent—her love of color, texture and composition—might be more suited to graphic or Web design than to a position in the service industry. Both industries were hiring—and certification in design was not any more intensive than in the field she chose. It's essential to remember that, when looking at your work self, you must consider your past, present, and future—what gives you satisfaction, what brings you success, what direction will enhance your life. Jeanne didn't consider any of this. She simply made an unexamined decision to do something different.

How does this relate to branding?

We take a lot of things about ourselves for granted. Lots of people are good managers or excellent communicators or highly proficient in functionality or adept at streamlining budgets or excellent at organizing the chaotic. You might ask yourself who really cares if you find an inaccuracy that slipped by ten other people or saved the company money when you switched to ergonomic work stations or sold more than your quota in a given month. That's your job. What's so unique about that?

No one needs to remind you that it's a competitive job market, and grabbing a hiring manager's attention is harder than it's ever been. That's why personal branding makes sense.

Branding turns the ordinary into the extraordinary. Let's take a look at the most popular brand on social networks: Starbucks.[11] When you think about a cup of coffee, maybe the ingredients come to mind: coffee and water, possibly some cream and sugar. If you really love coffee, you might rhapsodize about the aroma. But Starbucks has really delved into the essence of a cup of coffee. In fact, the company has discovered the full potential of a cup of coffee—lattes, cappuccinos, frappuccinos, macchiatos, mochas. Starbucks has turned the ordinary into something extraordinary.

We want you to think like Starbucks—or at least rethink how you see your work self. We asked Charlie Greene, a recently retired vice president of Trading Systems Development at NYSE Euronext, about his personal brand. Initially he looked puzzled, until we asked, "What were you known for at the Exchange?" He said: "I had a knack for making complex projects simple."

> I am the product of a Catholic-school upbringing, so early in life I learned how to pay attention and listen. As an adult, when I would go to a business meeting, that's what I did. I paid attention. Then I would ask a lot of questions. Not questions for the sake of asking questions; real questions, like How-does-this-get-done type of questions. I knew if I didn't understand what the leads were talking about, the people I managed wouldn't understand it either. So I asked questions until I understood thoroughly. Then I communicated this information to my team in plain English. At first, I did this instinctively. Eventually, as I was asked to oversee more complex projects, I realized this habit or instinct (or whatever it was) is what I was beginning to be known for in the company. Throughout my career, I made sure I got better at turning complex stuff into understandable implementations.[12]

This insistence on simplicity became part of Greene's personal brand. It didn't happen overnight, but nothing of real substance happens that way anyhow. Instead Greene recognized that there were certain core competencies his company valued, and he built his reputation around them. Maybe you complete projects ahead of schedule. Maybe you generate new leads, even in a downturned economy. Maybe you know how to save the company thousands on office supplies. Whatever it is that makes you stand out, that makes you a go-to person, that's the capability you want to build on and leverage. Write a brief mission statement about who you are, and see if you can make that your personal brand going forward.

If you are a newcomer to the job market, you might be wondering what you can possibly leverage as part of your personal brand. It's a little more difficult to do at this point in your career, but there are some capabilities that are part of your nature or temperament. Perhaps you are highly organized or analytical or reliable or generous or a dynamic personality—or just plain cooperative (a highly underrated competency). You don't need a full-fledged career to see certain patterns in your life; just a little self-reflection. These are competencies you want to highlight as you develop a personal brand. In the workplace, it's all about building on your strengths—not your weaknesses.

What about the real you?

With all this emphasis on self-examination, you might be thinking that your strengths are just half of the story; that you also have some real weaknesses—and they are just as much a part of the whole shebang as your strengths. Maybe you have struggled with a bad case of analysis paralysis or procrastination or social phobia your entire life, and you talk about it incessantly in the hope that one day you will overcome it. That's all legitimate. You should work on personal defects. Just do it quietly—with your therapist, your minister, your significant other, or a close friend. Personal defects are a private matter, and they are interesting and valuable only when they have been turned into strengths.

Which brings us to how this all ties in with social media: Just in case you need reminding, the Internet is a public forum. All of your likes and dislikes, musings, online chatter, and interaction with cohorts are accessible to those who may want to go to the trouble of finding out those colorful particulars. People sometimes forget this in their enthusiasm, sleep deprivation or after one too many beverages.

They broadcast unflattering portraits of themselves. And it can cost you a job, and sometimes even your reputation.

Brett Goodman, a recruiter for EdisonLearning, Inc., told us how he nixed an applicant, a very talented IT guy, because during the vetting process he encountered, without even trying, more than he bargained for:

> Just recently I needed to hire a User Support Technician. He made a junior mistake. I was really interested in him, but when he sent his resume he also included links to all the Web-sites he created, including his personal Website. I went to his personal Website and I found out a slew of information about him. Really none of this made a difference to me and I even thought he was kind of interesting, overall. But I got the impression from his personal Website that he didn't like too many people—and I drew a conclusion that this guy might not work too well with others. So even though this guy's Web-building skills were excellent, he knocked himself out of the running because we got more information than we needed.[13]

You already know about the danger of posting explicit photographs from Saturday night's beer-pong party. There's no need to remind you of avoiding that indiscretion, but this example points to the more subtle trails we leave when indulging personal negativity on the Internet. The applicant probably wasn't aware of the message he was sending. As Goodman said, it was a "junior mistake"—the mistake of thinking everyone thinks like you.

In Erik Qualman's book, *Socialnomics,* the author cites a case about a mother of three who has a friend who is questioning whether she is ready for children. The friend tells the mother that she is "the most with-it person that I know," and goes on to say that, "it seems like your kids are all that you can handle." The friend went on to tell her that she came to this conclusion based on the status updates that the mother had been posting on her social media page.[14] The young woman didn't realize the impression she was making, whining about the travails of motherhood, and the message she was sending out about her personal brand.

We are not suggesting that you must depict yourself exclusively in pure Pollyanna prose when you are online; some things need to be communicated that are not particularly pleasant—for the good of all parties concerned. But we are suggesting you examine everything you write about yourself and others. It should be rational and decent. Ask yourself before you commit it to print: Is it harmful to you or to others? What kind of message are you sending out to the world? Does it enhance or detract from who you are? Would you stand by it if it were on the front page of the *New York Times?* Heather McBride-Morse, an HR manager at a Fortune 500 Information Management and Systems company, said: "It's more about managing your information. You have to remember that whatever you say on a public forum reflects positively or negatively on you, so that's your brand. It doesn't matter where you're putting your brand, you're still putting your brand out there."[15]

Once you have made the decision to practice some self-censoring, you can proceed to building a personal online brand that will clarify your objectives and move you in the direction you want to go. Don't worry, you can be authentic without doing damage to yourself or others. All you have to do is keep the conversation productive. We agree with Newell Rubbermaid's Mike Rickheim that the best networkers are those who know how to blend the professional and personal well. Your online activity may be confined to one site or it may be scattered far and wide, but think about everywhere you spend time online and ask yourself what you are saying about your personal brand.

There's a reason Dale Carnegie's seminal 1936 business book, *How to Win Friends and Influence People,* has sold millions of copies. It's an ode to human decency in the marketplace, a reminder to keep your values in the midst of competition—playful or otherwise. Carnegie's book is still relevant today, even in a digital world. Do not lower your human decency standards just because you are online. Leave the "This Sucks" comments to those who are getting paid for them and/or the ornery, and keep your social communication valid, friendly, trustworthy, and informative. If you do have a legitimate complaint—perhaps you've been to Dell Hell and back—by all means, voice it, but don't act like a raving lunatic.

So what is fair game when it comes to engaging in social media and using it as a personal branding tool? Besides portraying yourself in the best light, consider a few more things, such as, be clear about your **interests** without being overzealous; engage in conversations where there is friendly **give-and-take**; add value to your content by **sharing** relevant information and perks by alerting others to events and other happenings; **network** with colleagues in a community or trusted network; **join** industry groups to learn about career opportunities; send out a **cohesive message**; have a sense of **humor**; recognize that, in most cases, "**less is more.**" Let's elaborate on these aspects.

Interests: In the movie *The Social Network,* the Mark Zuckerberg character tells the Sean Parker character that the Facebook crew assembled in Palo Alto lives and breathes code; "Parker" nods in approval and says he wouldn't have it any other way. Living and breathing code is not atypical for a lot of geeks, but, unless you are working for a demanding start-up that expects 24/7 participation and commitment, it's not a bad idea to come across as a more balanced human being. Whether you are rhapsodizing about fly fishing on the Big Horn River, all-night Call of Duty videogame-fests, rejuvenating yoga retreats in the Caribbean, or rain-soaked golf outings in Scotland, try to broaden your online portrait with some information that also says you are interested in your career. Find the right balance. This is equally true if your musings fall into the other camp—the camp of no interest in anything but self. If most of your blogs are of the navel-gazing variety, then broaden your outlook. Venture into some online communities that pique your curiosity. Include others. If you proceed slowly, you will quickly determine how you can contribute to the conversation. *Suggestion:* Google your name to see what digital impression you're creating. If you come across particularly lopsided in one area, realign your data for a more robust online profile by offering help to others, adding insight to an area of special interest, discussing your work, or recognizing others' achievements.

Give and take: What is particularly appealing about social media is that it's no longer a one-sided conversation. Instead it can be a creative or disruptive interchange of ideas and information and even a powerful collaborative tool. It is up to you how you participate. We asked Mike Troiano, principal at Holland-Mark (a Boston-based strategic marketing firm), who is ranked in the top 1 percent of the most influential people on Twitter, how he uses social media to brand himself. Troiano said: "Tactically speaking, I use it all. I don't really distinguish among social marketing tactics (tweets, status, etc.). My focus is less on the delivery mechanism, and more on delivering something of use to the people I'm connected to ('content'), sharing my authentic responses to whatever's happening around me ('persona') and engaging with those same people in a mutually beneficial dialogue ('rapport')."[16] *Suggestion:* Try participating on a forum. Carolyn Rice, a director of Talent Management at Kellogg's, said, "I think it's important that candidates have an online presence. I am too busy to write a blog, but I comment on them. I am interested in keeping abreast of what is happening in my field, so even if I don't want to create my own blog, I have the opportunity to read what others are thinking and writing and I can comment on it. This is not time-consuming and it keeps me updated."[17]

Sharing: There's a precept in the digital world that says WIIFM (What's In It For Me?) should form the basis of every Internet marketing plan. In one the "commandments" of *The Social Media Bible,* Lon Safko and David Blake said, "Thou shalt always have a strong WIIFM: This is always the most important commandment. Whether it's SEO, SEM, e-mail, Web pages or a hard copy brochure, your marketing message always has to have a strong 'What's In It For Me.'"[18] When building your brand, you should think like a marketing professional, too, every time you update or tweet. If you want digital engagement, ask yourself, What's In It For Them? To tap into Troiano's expertise again: "There are two kinds of people in the world: relationship people and transaction people. Transaction people don't want to leave anything on the table. They meet with you when it serves their interests. They have an agenda when they call. They become inaccessible when your ability to help them wanes. Relationship people recognize the value of associations. They see the strength in large networks of weak ties. They are always willing to help—to talk, refer, have coffee, whatever—and they expect the same in return."[19] *Suggestion:* Just to get a better balance, practice giving away exclusively for a few weeks. See what kind of response you get. This might mean adding links or photos or video to posts; making valuable contributions via comments or blogs; offering discounted tickets or coupons to a faithful following or friends; clicking on a positive customer review on Amazon and saying it was "helpful"; alerting the troops to a career fair. Nurture engagement. Give away more than you take.

Network, network, network: There's a theory in social media called the 1:50 principle, which states that everyone knows at least 50 people and each one of these 50 people knows an additional 50 people, so even as your circle widens by degrees of separation, your network becomes large enough to create new opportunities. In essence, you can improve your visibility—or personal brand—the wider your circle is and the "weaker" your ties. Because virtual connections are easier to maintain and foster than traditional connections, you can build a strong online presence by engaging with layers of people—friends of friends of friends. Heather McBride-Morse said your online networking should become "a daily habit—part of building your brand and building your own sense of job security. Companies are not really able to give you that security for life. You're building it every day yourself."[20] *Suggestion:* Erik Qualman, author of *Socialnomics,* recommends, "You need to network, before you need a network."[21] Set aside 10 minutes every day for some type of online networking activity. Do it for at least three months and see what kind of results you get. Don't wait until the last minute to build a network or revamp your online profile. Lissa Freed, a vice president of human resources at Activision, said that type of online behavior is fairly transparent: "What I've seen is that, by and large, most of the LinkedIn profiles are bare bones, so you can tell when someone in the organization starts looking because they beef up their profile...it's an indication when someone builds it out that they are much more seriously seeking [a new job] versus just wanting to stay connected."[22]

Join an industry group: If you are already virtually connected to hundreds of online friends and your LinkedIn connections are topping 500, joining another community may merely contribute to a serious case of information overload. But, if you are at the initial stages of broadening your social networking capabilities, by all means join an industry group or online community. These groups often post job leads and inside information. It's also good exposure to industry jargon, a valuable tool when revamping the keywords in your resume.

You have to start somewhere when you first start participating in social media, and as Kellogg's Rice said: "Everyone starts with zero contacts. You have to be patient and build them."[23] *Suggestion:* Follow targeted companies on Facebook or Twitter. Familiarize yourself with the industry and pay attention to all discussion regarding specific skills and company culture. These are important aspects of the hiring process. Offer suggestions and comments when you have something of value to add to the conversation. Just remember to put your best foot forward, even in the most benign or innocent exchanges. Set up a Twitter account to talk about your skills or work interests—in 140 characters at a pop. Use keywords so searches can find you, and, as Eric Kaulfuss, a talent director at CIGNA, said, "Don't put anything online that you wouldn't want a prospective employer or your current employer to see."[24]

Send a cohesive message: If your foray into social media was initially helter-skelter, now is the time to pull together your message and personal brand. Start with the obvious: If you have five or six blurry photos uploaded on a variety of sites, get one decent photograph and pull your profiles together that way. If damage control is necessary, start providing content that at least balances the more negative commentary. If some core competencies are more important in your industry than others, then make sure you are on board with these as well. Come across as an industry insider. *Suggestion:* Examine what all your innumerable online affiliations say about you, and use links to pull all your online activity together. Heather Huhman recommends: "Be Consistent: Linking your tweets to Facebook and other updates is a simple way to make your brand more cohesive and to update all of them more often. Have a message and communicate it to your audience. Stay on message and 'in character'—your brand should be reflected in person, online, in and out of the office."[25]

Humor: One of the main attractions of social media is that it's fun. So much fun that we've created innumerable initialisms to account for all our online hijinks: LOL, ROTFL, BWL, to name a few. Laughter is good medicine in any situation—whether at home or in the workplace—but we do have to proceed with some caution. Ask yourself if it's appropriate before you blast the "Trunk Monkey" video on YouTube to your colleagues or post an irreverent joke on

Facebook. Humor is good; cruelty and intolerance are not. *Suggestion:* First and foremost, know your audience. It is not difficult to inadvertently offend another person's sensibility or create an enemy by making another person the butt of your inconsiderate joke. Use humor wisely and it will do more for your brand than anything else: As David Hanscom said in a tweet on October 25, 2010, "Laughter is the shortest distance between two people."

Less is more: Exuberance for the new may have created a monster in disguise when you first ventured into social media. We heard time and again from Fortune 500 professionals that it's better to be thoughtful by targeting your online branding efforts than to spread yourself so thin that your reckless meanderings add up to an incoherent mess. Erik Qualman, author of *Socialnomics,* recommends, "When branding yourself online or building an online presence, don't try to boil the ocean. Meaning, don't feel you need to be on every digital tool (blogs, wikis, social networks, job networking sites, and so on). Rather focus on a niche you are passionate about and start on the few social networks important for that niche (for example, LinkedIn, YouTube) and after having some success and lessons, grow from there."[26] Determine which social media sites have the most value for your objective—which may be strictly for hiring purposes and networking or exclusively social-oriented. Laura Terenzi Khaleel, a director of Talent Acquisition Strategies at Pitney Bowes, recommends: "Start slow, start small, feel your way through it. As you get more comfortable, expand and extend your reach. Learn from others who know how to use it well. Because you can make mistakes and you can overuse it and you can put out information perhaps that you don't want out there."[27] *Suggestion:* Get an objective opinion and ask a friend how you can improve your LinkedIn profile so that it portrays a balanced, serious and viable candidate. Often a third party can spot a shortfall much more easily.

As in anything else, when venturing into the digital world it is better to proceed in a thoughtful manner than to have to retrace your steps or indulge in full-scale damage control. But regardless of where you are in your personal branding endeavor, keep in mind these suggestions Troiano offered:

1. Be authentic. It's hard to 'fake it' in social media, just because maintaining the façade takes too much trouble.
2. Listen first.
3. Curate the content you find useful by pointing it out to others.
4. Create content that adds value whenever and wherever you can.
5. Engage with people as people, not as institutions.
6. Recognize it's okay to ask for what you want if you do so in the context of the five preceding points.[28]

Chapter 2

Some Things Remain the Same, Sort Of

If you understand what you want or where you want to work or where you have a personal interest, those are the places to start—not the rapid-fire shotgun approach of everywhere.
—Laurie Byrne
Vice President, Global Staffing and Talent Development
Stryker Corporation

Social media has radically changed how we network and find new opportunities, but other aspects of the job search have remained fairly constant. No matter how strong your connections—virtual and otherwise—for most jobs you still have to do your research, create a resume, follow up, apply through an applicant tracking system, pass the telephone screen, show up for the face-to-face, make it through the background check, follow up some more, review the particulars, and, finally, make a decision to accept the offer; a decision that will dramatically change the next three, five, or even 10 years of your life.

That's a broad overview of the process, but actually the elements of finding a good job are almost as numerous as the elements on Mendeleev's periodic table. The good news is that, for the most part, the hiring process has evolved more deliberately and in many respects it is still more Web 1.0 or even pre-Web than it is Web 2.0. In other words, a lot of what you learned about the hiring process is still valid, but let's review the traditional job hunt in relation to how social media can enhance each stage of this process.

Without a doubt, the more focused your job search, the better your results. That's a given. In Chapter 1, we strongly urged you to get in touch with your work self. Not only does it enhance your personal brand, but it also helps you zero in on the type of job that will be a good fit for you. Why is this important? Because it's a waste of your time and the company's if you decide in six months that you are miserable at your new job and you leave (voluntarily or not).

You can avoid this scenario if you approach your new mission mindfully. Think about what interests you in the work world. Usually your work interests can be narrowed down to the skills that you are good at. Because it's next to impossible to be good at something that doesn't interest you, make sure your next job has plenty of, as Dan Pink says in *Drive,* "Goldilocks Tasks,"[1]—the kind of work that creates "flow." Make that a priority and you will be successful at your next job. Rodney Smith, author of *Stepping out of Self-Deception,* says in his book, "The point is to allow our interests, not our idealism, to lead our work."[2]

Examining your work self is the initial stage of your research. The next step is researching the job itself—as well as the company and the industry. And this is where Google makes your life very simple. Plug the name of the company into the Google search bar and in a click-second a full array of information pops up. Read everything. Then go to the company's Website and Career Page and read everything there. You can get a good sense of whether the company's culture aligns with your own values.

If the culture doesn't seem like a good fit, don't apply for the open position. Fitting in culturally at a company is just as important as having the right skills for a particular job.

How so? Let's take a look at what it's like to work at UPS, the second-largest employer in the United States (with a workforce that exceeds 400,000). Matt Lavery, the Corporate Workforce manager at UPS, described UPS as a "classic tortoise" (as opposed to a hare). He said, "You have to be willing to start at or near the bottom and work your way up."[3] Dan McMackin, the Public Relations manager at UPS, added, "It's a physically demanding job…. You need to work five nights a week—shorter shifts—but five nights a week. And you need to have a commitment to service. That sounds simplistic, but it's not. It's about serving people and we serve a whole bunch of them. We have 7 million daily customers. We ship 15 million packages a day."[4]

As appealing as UPS's perks are (promotion from within, job security, excellent benefits), if you get stressed by meeting tight deadlines or unscrambling messy logistics or you prefer to spend your evenings with the children, UPS might not be a good fit for you. And maybe you would prefer being a big fish in a smaller pond than the 400,000-plus at UPS. These are all serious considerations that you need to make about the culture of the company before you jump onboard.

Although there are no guarantees that everything you hear and read about a company beforehand will meet your expectations, you have never been in a better position to learn about the internal workings of a company. You can start with Google, then move to evaluating these companies on Facebook, Twitter, YouTube, blogs, micro-blogs, or within one of the many industry groups on LinkedIn. Read mainstream news articles about the company. Visibility has improved 100 percent since the days when you had to traipse off to the library to read a dry annual report to even get a sense of the type of business the company actually conducted.

At UPS, the human resource team is developing videos about how their senior leaders got their start at UPS—once again reinforcing the promotion-from-within culture—and they plan to post these videos on UPSjobs.com as well as the other large job boards. At American Family Insurance, Lisa Beauclaire, an HR specialist in Sourcing and Diversity, said the company is developing an AmFam Careers playlist on its American Family channel on YouTube.[5] Cindy Nicola, a vice president of Global Talent Acquisition at Electronic Arts, said the company keeps the conversation "light" and "entertaining" on Facebook for its 128,000-member community, but it is "leveraging the power of viral marketing" on the YouTube channel to "connect current employees, future employees, and brand ambassadors to life at EA." This is in addition to the company's blog *www.insideea.com* that "allows people to get under the skin and really see what life at our company is like."[6] At McGraw-Hill, Brian Jensen, vice president of Talent Acquisition, said, "We now added a Careers Tab on the Facebook page that has all the jobs on it. We have a job feed. Also on the main wall of the corporate Facebook page we get queried about jobs at McGraw-Hill or questions about the recruiting process. It's an avenue for a candidate to ask questions or seek guidance if they need it."[7]

To add to this corporate visibility, job candidates also have their own extensive networks to tap into when they want inside information on a company. Keith McIlvaine, a former global social media recruitment leader at Unisys, says younger professionals and recent college graduates sometimes prefer their own networks because they are often skeptical of companies "trying to control their brand," so "they want to be responsible for finding their own information."[8] Instead they prefer to call up a friend of a friend who interned at the company to get the low-down. But, regardless of what avenues you take while researching, it's essential that you study the targeted company thoroughly—before you even make contact with anyone there. Stan Weeks, a senior recruiting manager and college relations program manager at Weyerhaeuser, said, "Research is probably the single most important thing you can do to understand the company and understand what the company's future prospects are, what they've dealt with in the past, and what it is presently dealing with as well as where its hot spots are."[9] We agree; the better your research, the better your prospects.

The age of transparency is here. Companies have invested millions of dollars and dedicated significant resources to ensure that their brand is recognizable and visible. You don't want to walk into a job interview unsure of what the company is all about. That will probably disqualify you on the spot, which means you have to get organized before making contact with the company. Start creating files on your targeted companies. When you apply for a position, take notes and put it in the file. Review it often, just in case you get that random call and a hiring manager begins the prescreening process by quizzing you about why you are eager to work at ABC Company.

Lissa Freed, a vice president of Human Resources at Activision, said: "So many people don't take the time to research. Back to how you use the Internet, there is no reason that you should walk into any job and not be rich with content that you can readily find out there about a company, the industry, whatever. So many people just don't do their homework and there is no excuse for it because it is *all* there."[10]

Start by targeting five—at the most, 10—companies that are hiring. Start gathering your information. This approach is fairly simple if you stay focused. If the temptation hits you to use the shotgun method, resist it, even if you are feeling desperate about finding a new job. You don't want to have to go through this process all over again in six months or a year. This is just one more reason why it's always a good idea to find a new job while you still have your old job. You just make better decisions about where you want to go in your career when you are not under pressure.

Newell Rubbermaid's Mike Rickheim reinforced this idea when he said, "The best candidate in a hiring manager's eyes is the one who doesn't have to make a move. They are and have been gainfully employed and there's another employer who really wants to keep them, so it absolutely makes sense to engage in those conversations just to keep your options open. You are in a position of power as that 'passive job seeker.'"[11]

We know what you're thinking: Not everyone has that advantage, especially in light of the recent recession. In fact, many of you probably bought this book precisely because you are in the unenviable position of needing a job—today. We sympathize; the last two or three years were no fun for the many people who struggled to find a job, but, based on the feedback we got from the Fortune 500 HR professionals, we still think you should not jump into your next position without thoroughly researching your options and targeting a job that is a good fit for you. It may take a little longer than you're comfortable with. On average, finding a new job may take six months, but it's a worthwhile strategy to ensure that it's a good match. You will be so much better off in the long run.

Although not optimal, if you are taken by surprise by a reorganization or layoff, don't despair. Stay focused. As long as you have kept your network alive and well, you can tap into your connections—provided you know specifically what type of job you want and how you can be the solution to an employer's problem. When Chris Nutile, director of MediaLink Executive Search, was at Yahoo! Latin America, he was presented with a position he had to reject, so he went to his social network and announced he was coming back to New York and was looking for a contract opportunity.

> Actually I used an online solution, Ping.fm. Ping.fm or Hootsuite.com are sites that can be used to update all of your social network status messages at once. Facebook, LinkedIn, Yahoo!, AOL, they are all available. It can even tweet the update, and best of all, it does all that at once for you. You just set up an account, and provide permissions for the service to publish status updates across your various networks. It's a free Website and there is a dashboard on the Website. The Average Joe can figure it out. Some people might get concerned because you are putting in membership screen names and passwords to the various portals and Websites, but I think at this point people are getting more and more comfortable with those types of privacy issues.... I said I was coming back to New York and looking for contract recruiting opportunities as an "in-between" before deciding on my next permanent position. Within two days, my former colleagues at Google called me and made an offer to go back and ramp up hiring in the Business Development and Sales organizations.[12]

Staying plugged in to your network and clear about your next move can make the transition seamless, but remember to stay flexible and extend your reach as far as possible via social networks—go beyond the immediate and don't be afraid to tap into your weak ties. Your weak ties can be almost as helpful as your strong ties. Why? Because your weak ties don't usually know about the baseball glove you forgot to return to your still-miffed brother-in-law strong tie. And, as a result, these weak ties occasionally will help you more readily than your miffed brother-in-law.

We will emphasize again and again throughout *The Web 2.0 Job Finder* that it's better to find a new job before leaving your old job. Considering the economic climate, this suggestion may seem out of touch with reality. Many people are out of work, but the consensus of our Fortune 500 participants was clear: The employed are more sought after than the unemployed. Don't lose faith though. Although employers are eager to attract the passive candidate, rest assured, they also have no illusions about the impact this recession has had on the job market. CIGNA's Eric Kaulfuss said, "We understand the economic environment out there now…it's a question I hear from managers who are not working. They ask me if that's a problem, and I tell them it's not."[13]

The resume in 2011

As we were having our discussions with the Fortune 500 insiders, we couldn't help but wonder how the resume has changed in the Web 2.0 world. The good news is that while everything else may be swirling madly and changing rapidly in the job market, the resume hasn't really changed much—at least as far as content goes. And, as much as you like the fancy format, it is all about the content.

Yes, you still need a resume. Yes, it should have keywords on it that allow you to match up to specific, *open* positions. Yes, it should be clear, concise, grammatically correct, and accurate. Yes, it should showcase your accomplishments and skills. Yes, it should move you forward to your next job and challenge. David McMichael, an assistant vice president and manager of Staffing Strategies and Programs at SAIC, said, "I think the same information a prospective employer wanted to see 10 years ago, that same information still resonates today. That's what they're looking for when they try to gauge somebody's skill set via a resume."[14] Does that mean you can pull up your old resume, brush it off, and update it without considering Web 2.0? If it's in excellent shape, you might be able to avoid revamping it. But, before you upload your current resume to LinkedIn, consider what Fortune 500 participants said just in case there's room for improvement. Think of your resume as a living, breathing document that you will continually update as you target companies and apply to specific, open positions—your resume should always be a work in progress because you are going after specific jobs at specific companies and a one-size-fits-all resume will not do you justice.

The job you want

Now that you have given your next career move a good deal of thought—and you know what direction you want to go in—go to Google and search job postings for the position you want. Before you even start revising your resume, print the job postings out. Read them carefully.

Say you want to be a line manager in logistics. Go to the job boards—industry-specific and otherwise—and parse several job postings to get a good sense of how hiring managers view the job you are after. The more job postings you look at, the better your grasp. There's a lot of relevant information in job postings and if you make it a habit to review them carefully *before* you update your resume, they will help you:

- get a handle on the language the employer uses
- identify the keywords that are relevant to your specific job and industry, and
- assess what the company values.

Also when the same keywords appear again and again in the job postings from different companies, you know those keywords are core competencies that you *must have* to be qualified for that position. In addition, reading job postings is especially helpful to newcomers to the workforce. If you don't have the skills required for the position you are interested in, invest in getting them—sign up for a course or certification program. For instance, take a look at the following job posting for a **Regional Logistics Services Deployment Manager (Processes)**:

Regional Business Partnering Role
Individual Contributor Role (Strategic Role)
   ABC Company is a Global IT/Telco MNC with strong year-on-year growth
   and multibillion-dollar revenues. We offer many products and services to our

clients, and due to stable and rapid expansion, we are looking for a Regional Logistics Services Deployment Manager (Processes) to support us in a Global/Regional Initiative, which is redesigning the corporate approach in Logistics Operations.

Job description

Reporting to the regional director of Logistics, you will identify and generate opportunities for building a global supply chain, and drive implementation of projects in collaboration with clients and inside teams. You will participate in the creation and deployment of logistics service offerings, ensuring the deployment of highly effective logistics processes, capabilities, solutions, systems, and tools to operations, based on defined best practices and road maps.

Your other responsibilities include:

Manage customers and inside operational requirements to develop action plans for future capability deployment; support development of Sales Units customer logistics strategy and customer service offerings, in seamless cooperation with clients and logistics teams; manage deployment of programs and projects; implement capability and solutions; review and cascade current portfolio of capabilities, programs, and solutions.

The successful applicant

You must possess a Bachelor's degree with minimum of 10 years of related work experience and knowledge in logistics operations, process improvement, and implementation. You must possess knowledge of competitive models for import/export operations for product delivery and knowledge and experience in downstream logistics. You should possess excellent organizational, interpersonal, and communication skills, and work effectively in a highly diverse, global, multifunctional environment that works across multiple time zones. Project management skills/experience, i.e. Lead, Six Sigma or Kaizen, is highly advantageous.[15]

If you were to apply for this job, many of the words and phrases should appear on your resume (provided, of course, you actually have this type of experience). This is the language you need to know to get this job; these are the skills you need to have to be successful in this position. Do you have to match up word for word, 100 percent? According to Megan Dick, a manager of human resources at Cameron, "There is no such thing as a perfect match."[16] But a close match is what most companies expect.

Keywords may sound like old news—so Web 1.0—but they are uniquely important in today's job market. How important are keywords in a Web 2.0 job hunt? Pitney Bowes' Khaleel said keywords are "critical, critical, critical."[17] The job market is all about search, and search depends on keywords.

Here's what Jim Gattuso, director of Staffing and Recruitment at CSC, said about how keywords impact search: "The basic resume—the format and the content of the resume—is pretty much the same as it's been for certainly the last 30 or 40 years. It is normally a chronological representation of someone's work history with some sort of a summary objective or objective statement at the front that contains work history and educational history and sometimes a small amount of personal information about some groups or affiliations that the person may have, but I think what may have changed is that lots of candidates may have become a little more savvy to the fact that their resume in the original format may never be seen by a pair of human eyes. It's going to be received, scanned, and through keyword search people will find their resume or not find their resume."[18]

If you just spent hours, or days even, writing your resume—and fooling with indents, rules, bullets, and typeface—the fact that your resume may not be viewed by human eyes may vex you. It's bad enough that you have to condense your extensive work experience to one or two pages; now you find out a computer scanner is deciding if you make it past the first round.

What to do? Use keywords. Parse the job posting for the open position very carefully. If the job posting says you need to have advanced Microsoft Excel skills (and you have them), make sure that information is on your resume. If it says you need to develop PowerPoint presentations, put that on your resume. If it says you need certain certifications, don't apply unless you are certified (or at least in the process of pursuing these certifications). Of course, not every company handles a submitted resume this way, but the larger companies do. They have to. They get an enormous number of resumes per day and these resumes have to be scanned and tracked.

With all this emphasis on keywords, it might be a temptation to fudge a few. Actually, according to NYSE-Euronext's Charlie Greene, a hiring manager is practiced at detecting whether a candidate is qualified for a job within about 15 minutes of a face-to-face interview. Going that far in the hiring process is a waste of everyone's time if you're not qualified. Better to recognize early in the job hunt what skills are necessary to do a particular job and do a crash course—at night school, while at a contract or freelance project, or at some other certification program or college. There really aren't too many ways around getting the qualifications you need for a particular job. Not that people haven't tried.

Some job seekers were so hell-bent on making it past that first round that they loaded their resumes with every relevant keyword by hiding them in a white font. That way the scanner picked up the keywords and the resume was brought to the hiring manager's attention. Ryder's Kirk Imhof said, "There were ways early on for individuals to hide words in a resume so that when you did a keyword search a white font word against a white background was never seen—it was buried in your resume—but it was picked up by the search tool. And there were little tricks to make sure you had lots of keywords to ensure your resume would be pulled up. That doesn't really work well anymore."[19]

So how do you get your resume to stand out? One of the cardinal rules of writing *anything* is to know your audience. As far as writing a resume, you have to use the language of the employer (who wrote the job postings that the computer is scanning). And you have to have the qualifications—be a good match—for the job to which you are applying. You can simplify this process by understanding what's required. That's why it's so beneficial to read job postings for your particular field and position before you even attempt to write your resume. Even if the next job is a stretch for you (and it should be), know what's required, so you don't look like you're in over your head. Martin Cepeda, senior university recruiter at a Fortune 500 healthcare company, said, "Your resume needs to be specific to the job that you are applying for. If you are applying for 10 jobs, I would suggest creating up to 10 different resumes that are keyword-specific to those jobs. This would allow the recruiter to view a resume that highlights your specific transferable skills that are relevant to the job that he/she is recruiting for."[20] When writing your resume, keep this in mind: Although it is essential that you do a good job of presenting your skills and qualifications in a resume, this is not the most crucial aspect of the job hunt. Spend 20 percent of your time writing a targeted resume and 80 percent of your time forming a network and making a connection within your targeted company.

Your words matter—a lot

While the job hunt unfolds, make the employer's language yours by using their keywords. If you do match up well keyword-wise with the job posting and you decide to apply for the position, print the job posting and save it in your special file so that when an HR person calls you for a prescreening interview, you can speak specifically to the skills required for that job—every aspect of it (refresh your memory with the job posting right before your actual interview, too). Fortune 500 participants said again and again that you won't score any points if a hiring manager calls you on the telephone and you are clueless as to what company you reached out to. A thoughtful, targeted approach is your best strategy—always.

Just as keywords should be part of your arsenal when looking for a job, they also play an important role when companies cast their nets for prospective employees. Search is still king, even in the Web 2.0 world. Pitney Bowes' Khaleel said her company created a Search Engine Optimization [SEO] site earlier this year where all the company's job openings are pulled each night, and whenever "someone is in Google or any of the job aggregators—like Indeed.com or Simply Hired or Juju or any other search engine—whatever words they type up as keywords, we want our jobs to come up if it's a relevant search. That's why we have established a separate search completely and totally geared toward search engine optimization."[21] This suggests that companies are making an effort to learn your language too, which makes perfect sense in a social media landscape where *dialogue* is the name of the game.

Make their job easy

Put yourself in the recruiters' shoes. They see hundreds of resumes each day—especially at larger corporations. Finding a good fit between an open position and candidates takes time and resources. What you want to do is catch a recruiter or hiring manager's attention with your resume quickly. Don't worry if you haven't expounded on all your innumerable qualities; you'll have plenty of time to do that later—in the applicant tracking system or, if you are lucky, at the job interview. As far as your electronic resume goes, less can be more at this stage of the game. Try to be crisp and clear about your intentions. Ian Decker, a director of Talent Acquisition at MetLife, gave another reason to keep it brief: "I think there are many different theories about a resume. Should it be one page? Should it be two pages? What should be on it? I still think for a mid- to senior-level professional, a two-page resume with just enough to whet your appetite where you want some more is good. You don't want to put everything on the resume because then I don't have any reason to call you. You've already told me everything. But if you give me enough for me to say, 'Wow, this is great. I want to learn more,' then I am going to call you."[22]

So if you are just putting your resume together now, you may be wondering what the appropriate length is. Generally, for someone with fewer than five years' experience, a one-page resume is sufficient; for most others, a two-page resume is standard.

Obviously, in the Web 2.0 world, we are talking about electronic resumes. During the initial application process, paper resumes have almost become irrelevant. Karen Bradbury, assistant vice president of Talent Management Strategies at Unum, said, "You need to think about the workload of a recruiter and just what a company has to keep track of in terms of applications and resumes and so on. If a company gets a paper resume, it's just three more steps that a recruiter has to take. It has to be scanned and in the system and matched to a job—and that's not a situation you want to be in as a recruiter or as a candidate."[23]

That doesn't mean you won't eventually need a paper resume. If your first introduction to a company is at a career fair or you are invited to a face-to-face interview, a hard-copy resume is expected. On the day of your interview, for instance, you may meet with several people who will want a hard copy of your resume when you speak to them. But, nowadays, most job applicants make their initial contact with a company via the Web or LinkedIn—and that means your resume is electronic. The point is to find out what the protocols are for the hiring process at whatever company you apply to—and then follow those protocols to the letter. It's part of making the hiring manager's job easy.

Your networks—social and traditional—are excellent resources for this type of information. If your targeted company has a Facebook page, ask about specific aspects of the hiring process. Make a connection with a recruiter on LinkedIn and ask for specifics. Tap into your colleagues from former jobs and ask them what they know about your targeted company. They may actually know someone who is working there and put you in touch with that person. But, before you proceed to that stage, you need to develop a strong resume, so let's cover some of its features.

Simple yet professional

A resume should comprise contact information, career objective, work history, education specifics, computer know-how or other relevant information (such as language fluency), and affiliations (sometimes relevant personal interests). Unless you work in the creative fields, those components form a standard resume, even in the Web 2.0 world. Without overstating the obvious, this information must be accurate. There are a lot of variables on a typical resume, and one or two elements can slip under the radar, so be careful. Read your resume twice—and then have an objective third-party proof it again—before you hit Send.

Keep the resume simple yet professional. Starting with the contact information, it should read: name, address, telephone number, and e-mail address. Provide a URL to your Website in this section, if it is relevant. For now, focus on content and be sure everything is accurate. Format, unless you are creative capital, is secondary.

Marie Smith
16 A Smith Street
Waldwick, NJ 07463
(201) 555-5555 (cell), mxzsmith@gmail.com

This is fairly straightforward, but, according to Fortune 500 HR managers, they have seen errors even in the contact information. Nowadays you **must** have an e-mail address; also it's a good idea to include only one telephone number. Chris Nutile, director, MediaLink Executive Search, said, "Always try to use a local phone number—some people move from San Francisco and they are still using their cell phone from

San Francisco. You know what, sign up for Google voice and get yourself a local phone number and have it forward to that cell phone. It is really important because as a recruiter I want to be sure the person definitely lives in that city in case relocation is not available and I want to know what I am dealing with."[24] Nutile also urges applicants never to use the company e-mail where they are currently employed. Your employer legally has the right to review e-mail sent on their system. Be sure to have a professional e-mail address (avoid cutiepieXO@hotmail.com). "My suggestion is always use a very professional, or appropriate, non-work e-mail address. So first name dot last name—get it now, because it may not be there in two months. Use Yahoo! or a Google e-mail account— Gmail is considered a little bit more cutting-edge—so that is a plus if you can get it."[25] Keep the type size of your name the same size as the rest of the contact information (boldface does work well in this section though).

Next create a career objective—a meaningful one, not a generic one—that says something about who you are and where you want to go. A career objective can have several names—professional summary, professional profile, focus statement, qualifications summary—but generally it's a two- or three-line encapsulation underneath your contact information that indicates the position you are applying for at the new company. The objective should contain plenty of targeted keywords. Is an objective necessary? Kellogg's Carolyn Rice said: "I like career objectives. On a resume without one, all you have is your history. If you want to do in your new job exactly what you were doing in your old job, then it's not necessary to have a career objective. I don't think that's the case with a lot of people though. When they move to another job, they are looking for a change. That change should be communicated in the career objective."[26]

So if you were looking for a new sales position, avoid generic objectives that read:

Seeking challenging and rewarding position in sales industry.

Instead write one that conveys skills while also pinpointing a specific open position at the company—with some relevant keywords, of course: *Sales and marketing professional—with proven track record of account acquisition, business development skills and ability to convey value proposition through management skills—seeks **Account Executive** position at ABC*

Company. Adept at responding to changing environment and implementing strategies optimizing profit and growth. That objective may seem like a mouthful, but it's much more focused and it uses language—and keywords—the employer can appreciate.

Your professional history—where you worked and what you did—is the crux of the resume. This is where you list, preferably in chronological order, the companies you worked for, the location of each company (and a brief description or URL for each company if it's not well-known), the time you worked there, and the title of your position, followed by a bulleted description of your accomplishments and skills.

Professional History:

XYZ Company (www.xyz.com)
New York, NY
Facilities Manager
1999 to 2010
- Created centralized construction and purchasing department, consolidating all construction and purchasing functions for procurement of goods and services nationwide.
- Managed retrofit of 200 retail locations and more than 50 new retail locations; handling design, construction, licenses, and permits from government agencies.
- Promoted from Assistant Purchasing Agent (2001) to Purchasing Agent (2005) to Facilities Manager (2007).
- Negotiated with vendors to establish nationwide programs for procurement of all construction materials, HVAC, architecture, general contracting, computer/communications and infrastructure as well as office equipment, resulting in 30-percent cost reductions.
- Established best practices; developing and distributing purchasing handbook detailing instructions on purchasing of all goods and services.
- Created centralized purchasing process for outfitting retails with materials necessary to open new business.
- Automated construction and purchasing department, using IBM Macola Systems, resulting in reduced costs and improved efficiency.

This is a bulleted description of what you did and what you know. Keep in mind a few things: First, it should *not* be a detailed description of your duties or responsibilities. Instead rephrase your material so it showcases your accomplishments, skills, and contribution; second, if you received a promotion, highlight this—it shows your company valued you as an employee; third, the company you worked for carries its own weight, even if it's not well known—if it's a growing and dynamic company, a short description or URL is always helpful to include; fourth, use keywords, especially ones that will be transferable to your next position; finally, how long you worked at a company matters—anything more than three years says to a future employer that you are a "loyal" employee. In fact, the longer at a company, usually the better—provided your resume doesn't suggest you sat in a cubicle for 10 years twiddling your thumbs.

Your professional history should address how your skills can help the prospective employer. Think of it this way: The new company has a problem and you are the solution to that problem. Whether you know it or not, no one else can do what you do, so rethink your skills. How are they unique to you? Renowned Choreographer Twyla Tharp, in *The Creative Habit,* said, "An awareness of your particular set of skills will tell you what sets you apart. When asked to explain his success, Billy Joel says, 'I have a job where I get to do the only things I'm good at doing. I can sing in tune. I can play an instrument. I can write songs. And I can get on stage and perform. I'm not a virtuoso at any single one. I'm competent and I do my job. But I'm in a field, the music industry, which sees this as extraordinary.'"[27] Take the opportunity in your Professional History section to convince a prospective employer that your skills are extraordinary—even if you are humble by temperament. Cast yourself in the best light; it's really just an attitude adjustment.

It was mentioned earlier that chronological resumes are the preferred format. Whereas skills resumes or functional resumes are useful for some professions—especially if you plan to continue to work independently—most hiring managers like a clear timeline, which the chronological resume provides. If you jumped around a lot or worked many contract jobs you may be tempted to downplay this fact with a functional resume if you are applying for a full-time position. We don't recommend it. Most hiring managers can see through that veil a mile away. Better to be straightforward and clear—there's nothing wrong with establishing from the get-go that "that was then, this is now," which places the resume squarely in the heart of Web 2.0.

Getting back to transparency in the Web 2.0 world, everyone has quick and deep access to information. Stay honest. Google can expose a lot of flaws, so it's better to meet everything head-on. PPG Industries'

Shannon Pelissero said, "I don't know if I would say the resume has changed. I think the job seeker has changed as a result of the Web 2.0 world because information is so readily available now that job seekers have changed their perception. If I found a candidate I liked, I could go on Facebook and search his or her name or I could go on LinkedIn and do the same. I could find out a lot about that person before I even talked to them. I think that has changed the job seeker's perception. For instance, they have to be more honest because all this information is readily available.... Also they can find out a lot about us, too."[28]

The last section of the resume should be reserved for credentials including degrees, certifications, language fluency, and computer know-how. If you graduated within the last five years or your work history is minimal or nonexistent, your education gets top billing, after the career objective and before the work history. Add a GPA if it is 3.0 or higher. Whether you are a college graduate or not, list any information in this section that tells the employer that you are a life-long learner: advanced classes, even night classes qualify, especially those that are relevant to the current position you are seeking. Your highest level of education should be listed.

The following sample resume will pull all these elements together, but first just a few words about layout and design. Unless you are a creative, don't sweat the design. Content is much more important, and the simpler your resume is, the better—strive for *compatibility.* MediaLink's Chris Nutile said, "Oftentimes PDFs or other forms of documents don't translate very well for an applicant tracking system because they have trouble parsing the information into the applicant database. My recommendation is to always use a Word document." [29] We suggest Microsoft Word 97–2003 (some companies don't have the latest version of Word). Electronic resumes have a penchant for disfigurement (indents are especially tricky), and, in most cases, your resume eventually will be pulled apart in an applicant tracking system and automatically converted to plaintext. The following resume is simple yet professional.

Mary Zella Smith
100 Smith Street
Smithtown, CT 00000
(000) 000-0000, URL (if you have a Website)
MS1010@verizon.net

Career Objective: *Highly skilled Line Manager/Negotiator seeks Operations Director position. Worked in all aspects of Shipping—from broker/dealer to traffic. Adept at handling distribution logistics, building revenue, and ensuring high standards from pick-up to delivery.*

Professional History:
ABC Company (*www.abccompany.com*)
New York, NY
Senior Account Executive
2003 to Present
* Manage 50 accounts, with a net profit ranging between $300,000 and $500,000.
* Structure client-specific shipping programs to address seasonal pricing and volume and transit requirements while enhancing operational controls.
* Provide service to clients while allowing customization of transportation and logistics needs.

DEF Company
New York, NY
Vice President
1998 to 2003
* Provided cost-sensitive and competitive pricing for customers in all aspects of international transportation from import/export, LCL/FCL coverage.
* Managed staff of 15 and promoted staff development through continuing education and enhancing knowledge of competitive marketplace.
* Ensured regulatory and compliance measures were met within global guidelines.
* Reduced costs by 10 percent by implementing best practices.
* Optimized international supply chain logistics network with multiple distribution centers.

JKI Company
Hoboken, NJ
FCL Development Manager
1996 to 1998
* Developed and maintained relationships with ocean freight carriers.
* Clinched contracts by providing thorough updates on current market trends to customers.

- Reported updated information on carriers' status in ocean freight surcharges.
- Monitored key accounts and increased sales revenue by $500,000.
- Maintained extensive communication with clients and overseas offices.

LMO Shipping Company
New York, NY
1988 to 1996
Assistant Line Manager
- Managed all aspects of international traffic, bookings and sales in Relay Department.
- Coordinated and negotiated ocean rates; scheduled, routed and traced export freight shipments.
- Negotiated volume deals with brokers, shippers and non-vessel operating common carriers.
- Supervised operations of 13 U.S. offices and reported to VP while overseeing order processing, pricing and customer service. Promoted to Assistant Line Manager in 1992.
- Created and analyzed marketing, financial and sales reports.
- Quoted pricing policies, tariffs, and export rates while establishing all tariff and time/volume rates for major export trade lanes.
- Communicated with sales staff regarding delays, scheduling and customs issues.
- Developed bid proposals, negotiating sales and service contracts for key accounts.

PQR Company
New York, NY
1986 to 1988
Traffic Manager
- Coordinated export consolidation to Far East while documenting bookings, bank transactions, follow-up shipments, and export records. Promoted to Traffic Manager in 1987.
- Solicited U.S. importers for international steamship freight transportation service.
- Negotiated rates, terms and conditions with Far East and European offices.

Education, language, computer know-how, and affiliations:
- World Trade Institute of Export; Traffic, Documentation, Letters of Credit Courses—1983
- State University of New York at Stony Brook; B.A. Sociology—1979
- Former Member of Women's Traffic League
- Fluent in English and Hebrew; extensive travel in Europe and Israel
- Proficient in Microsoft Office: Excel, PowerPoint, Word, Visio, Access, Outlook
- Proficient in Internet research. LinkedIn profile: http://www.linkedin.com/in/maryzellasmith.

The preceding sample is an outcome-based resume, with emphasis on the applicant's achievements and promotions. Verifiable numbers and accomplishments will always make more of an impression than hype. Be sure the language in your resume suggests that you are a doer and not a paper pusher. Nouns are good, verbs are better—specific numbers and promotions sing. Your information, however, should not compromise a former employer.

Resumes have a style of their own, so avoid personal pronouns and start your bulleted information with verbs (where the *I* is implied) and end each line with a period if it's a complete sentence. Use present-tense verbs for your current position and past-tense verbs for former positions. Because of space limitations, it is perfectly acceptable to drop articles (*the, a*), even though the sentence may sound clipped.

Compatibility is an issue for electronic resumes submitted via e-mail. Most hiring managers are tolerant of a few snafus, but if it's totally garbled, a hiring manager might just skip over your resume. You can avoid this situation by having two versions of your resume: a standard version similar to the preceding sample and a plaintext version. If you need to convert your resume to plaintext to make it more compatible, it's fairly simple:

- Once in your e-mail, retrieve your original resume from Microsoft Word.
- Go to File and hit Save As.
- In the Save As window that pops up, rename your original resume P-text (your last name).
- Underneath the File Name bar, go to Save As Type. Click on the arrow and then scroll down and highlight Text Only. Then hit Save.
- When the warning pops up that your formatting will be lost, hit Yes.
- Complete the conversion by closing the document and then reopening it in Word so you can readjust the margins and clean up any formatting.

As mentioned earlier, if you are applying through an applicant tracking system, the conversion is often automatic, but it's still good to know how to convert it to plaintext yourself just in case. As already mentioned, Word 2003 documents are most compatible, so avoid PDFs or other word-processing programs. Once again, make the hiring manager's job easy.

There are exceptions, however, to the general rule of using Word documents exclusively for resumes and they apply to creative capital. Creative jobs often require creative solutions, so resumes often veer away from the standard resume and instead are either interactive or, at the very least, linked to Websites. Activision's Lissa Freed said, "In the creative world, more and more resumes are linked to Websites where you can view a portfolio...just the ability to create a Website with your content there versus hauling in a big portfolio. I see it more in the creative fields."[30] Take a look at Paula Cuneo's resume at *www.wix.com/paulacuneo/resume*.[31] She posted the link to her resume on her Facebook page. She does an excellent job of personal branding.

If you cannot decide whether an interactive resume is the right medium for you, take into consideration what Lisa Beauclaire, a sourcing and diversity specialist at American Family Insurance, said: "Someone inquired about our social media digital marketing department as we were getting that rolling and they had quite an interactive resume. It is impressive when you see something a little bit different, but we haven't had to make decisions on video resumes yet because it's so new. I do know (just from getting into the branding and video that we're starting to do), you still have to be—communication-wise—really polished in order to do it. So if you're going to do it, do it right. Some people might not present themselves well in video."[32]

Applicant tracking systems (ATS)

Nearly all large companies use applicant tracking systems. You've seen the recruiting software when you apply for a position on the job boards and you are redirected to the company Website via Brass Ring, Taleo, RecruitSoft, or PeopleSoft (to name a few).

You may roll your eyes when you are redirected because an ATS usually means that in addition to uploading your resume you will be spending from 30 minutes to an hour filling out job-specific questions, which are designed to ensure the company receives both the information and the focus it wants. Weyerhaeuser's Stan Weeks said, "We use a cutting-edge system. We use Taleo, a system of choice for most companies. When we see a resume, they all come across and look the same way. Resumes are pulled on required questions that the candidate has to answer and keyword searches."[33]

An ATS acts as a central database for a company's recruiting efforts. It usually means that you can only apply for specific open positions (unsolicited resumes are not welcome). In 99.9 cases, applicants must go through the ATS before being considered a viable candidate. Here's how CSC's Jim Gattuso explains the process: "When an applicant applies for a specific position or wants to be considered formally as a candidate, we ask the applicant to go into our career site and submit some information and include a resume. We also gather additional information, including some voluntary disclosures, some demographic information.... We ask the applicant to go through, what I call, the front door, through our career site.... Eventually every applicant goes through the front door and into the applicant tracking system."[34]

Recruiting software helps companies streamline their hiring process by tracking candidates. For companies, the software makes data easier to sort and retrieve: It filters candidates by matching data against job requirements, it ranks candidates, it accelerates communication with applicants, and it enables companies to ask job-specific questions regarding experience, skills, and interests for each position posted. For applicants, it allows a more thorough picture of your capabilities than a one- or two-page resume ever could.

But it also requires that you commit some time to the application process. You cannot rush through because your communication skills are on display and you can be knocked out of the running if you handle this prescreening stage carelessly. At PPG,

"Candidates are able to attach up to 20 documents in their application, so you get the cover letter, the resume, the letters of recommendation, the awards they've won. It can be overkill and sometimes I think you hurt yourself more than you help yourself with that."[35]

An ATS also discourages candidates who may not be serious about the company—those who use a spray-and-pray methodology for applying to job postings—because filling out all that information is a time-consuming venture. The downside for companies is that an ATS may chase away very qualified candidates—those gifted engineers who aren't good spellers or those computer wizards who speak English as a second language or those dynamic personalities who are just too busy to expend a few hours on an iffy prospect. It's a challenge to devote this much time to something when there may not be a reward. But if you are seriously interested in the targeted company or you do receive some encouragement to go to the company Website from a recruiter, then give this part of the process everything you have—while still remaining concise and accurate. And then follow up. E-mail a recruiter—if you have his or her name—or contact an insider that you may have found a connection to. Do not be a pest, but by all means express your interest. Say in your e-mail, "I just submitted my application via your ATS and I was wondering if you can give me any other advice on the hiring process."

Regardless of the fact that most large companies insist that you apply through the ATS, it can be a disincentive to many. Lisa Beauclaire of American Family Insurance said her company wants to capture applicants in a less intensive manner. "We're looking at some systems, in addition to the applicant tracking system, where people can submit interest in American Family, without actually applying. Some people choose not to go to our ATS because of the time commitment, so this new option would create more of a talent community to go along with social media. People could just opt in and leave their contact information, which could simply be their name, number, e-mail address, and we can keep in contact with them."[36]

Set aside some quiet time to devote to the ATS because a lot is riding on your thoroughness. And be prepared to answer specific questions clearly and briefly. Stan Weeks explains, "The way our applicant tracking system is set up for compliance is that we base our position on several required questions. The applicant applies and he or she has to answer certain questions, such as, 'Are you proficient in Excel, yes or no?' If they press yes, they come across as a viable candidate. If they press no, then they don't come across as a viable candidate and we don't have to look at them because they don't match the minimal skill set of the position. If 300 people apply, and 290 don't know Excel, then we only have to look at the 10 that do. If all 300 have Excel, we have to look at every single candidate."[37]

It is much easier to expend the energy an applicant tracking system requires when you have received encouragement from a recruiter to "stay in touch," but regardless of what point in the job search you encounter a company's applicant tracking system, just remember that you have to climb the ATS wall to get to some of the better jobs in the marketplace. And sooner or later, if you plan to work at a large or mid-size company, you will have to go through the "front door." Things may change in the future though. SAIC's David McMichael said:

I think the power of social media will make a prominent impact on not only how people search for jobs but also on how they apply to jobs. Right now companies are becoming increasingly proficient at leveraging social media for employment branding and to locate and attract talent, but there isn't much discussion about using social media to simplify the application process. Why not? Today job seekers are burdened by a complicated application process and employers are frustrated by low career site conversion rates. Insert the highly flexible capabilities of the social Web into that picture and we discover a huge opportunity for a practical solution—you apply to jobs via your LinkedIn profile or some other social profile in a matter of seconds. As this type of technology becomes a reality, we may see companies sprinting to implement.[38]

The crucial paragraph

A lot of effort has been expended up to this point—research, targeting five companies (maybe a few more), examining whether the ATS will be part of the hiring process—but you are still at the early stages of your job hunt. A crystal-clear resume that resounds with your accomplishments and skills is a good beginning, but now you have to write that crucial paragraph; not the cover letter, but the elevator pitch about your qualifications. Although many Fortune 500 employers said the cover letter was not as important as it once was—simply because there are so many other calling cards in the Web 2.0 job market—you still need to write a short paragraph about what you have to offer. This summary is the paragraph that will eventually become part of your cover letter. It is also the paragraph you will memorize in the event that you run into someone at the grocery store or on the soccer field or while grabbing a cup of coffee at Starbucks and you want to let them know that you are available. And this may be the paragraph you recite in the event that you receive a telephone screen from an interested employer.

This 30-second pitch should be a brief encapsulation of your skills and qualifications and emphasize the skills you want to use in your next job:

> I have five years' experience as an executive assistant at XYZ Company, working for the vice president of Marketing and the group director of Business Development. Working in the fashion industry, I am highly adept at extensive scheduling of calendar activities, responding to clients' requests, monitoring promotions, directing editors to the appropriate channel, onboarding new hires and reconciling expense reports as well as providing daily support to the Marketing team with my highly proficient skills in Excel, PowerPoint, Microsoft Office, and Adobe.

Write this summary now—and then wait until you have finished information-gathering before even attempting to write the cover letter. Why? In the Web 2.0 job market, the focus has shifted in the cover letter. You are no longer the star; instead you are the second paragraph. The first paragraph of your cover letter is about the employer—and why you want to work specifically for that employer. But, right now, you will need a summary. Spend some time thinking about who you are and where you want to go, and then write four or five lines that convey how you are uniquely qualified to add value to whatever job you target.

Cindy Nicola, vice president of Global Talent Acquisition at Electronic Arts, said, "I am seeing people move away from cover letters,"[39] and Vincent Taguiped, a manager of recruitment at a Fortune 500 media company, agrees. In the digital environment, "You should *always* be putting your best foot forward," he said.[40] So create a summary of who you are and what you have to offer before making contact with a company. The approach will attest to your preparedness—a highly valued skill in a tumultuous marketplace.

Chapter 3

Tapping Into the Hidden Job Market Via LinkedIn

If you look at LinkedIn, there are people who normally don't go on job boards or people who don't normally post for jobs on corporate Websites that we've been able to find and either create relationships with them or find people who have relationships with them, and it's enabled us to spread our net a little wider.

—Eric E. Kaulfuss
Talent Director, Talent Optimization
CIGNA

The hidden job market—those unadvertised jobs that are filled by word of mouth—is alive and well; in fact, it never died, not even during the recent economic downturn. Companies never stop hiring completely—unless they are losing a lot of business—but they do hire differently when times are lean. Instead of rushing to fill every vacant position, employers hire slowly, proceed with caution, and strategically turn to their own employees for help when the economy contracts.

The Fortune 500 hiring managers we spoke to validated this. Generally they said between 20 and 30 percent of their new hires result from their own employee referral programs—and these are just the new hires they can track.

Many said the percentage is probably higher because many new people come on board through more informal networking—the kind of conversations that don't show up in an applicant tracking system, such as, "Hey Mike, I heard they're hiring in Risk Management. You should shoot Terry Smith an e-mail."

Employers prefer to hire people they "know" because, as Met Life's Ian Decker said, "Obviously you get better candidates when someone who works at the company gives the name of somebody he or she knows. Typically that person doesn't want to refer someone who is unqualified because it's not a good reflection on the person who did the referring."[1] Although the Fortune 500 employers we spoke to vet all prospective employees thoroughly, it's added insurance when a new candidate comes on board as a result of a recommendation by a current employee. The trust factor—a key component of any business transaction—improves immeasurably when familiarity enters the equation.

You may be thinking this is all well and good, but what do you do if you don't know anyone at the targeted company where you're applying? That's the beauty of social networking. You can leverage new connections and tap into this hidden job market much more quickly via social media. The best place to start, according to our Fortune 500 experts, is to build a robust LinkedIn profile that showcases your professional qualifications. But before we delve into LinkedIn, let's look how the employer views the hidden job market, so you can best position yourself and make the most of your outreach efforts.

Why networks work

It can take anywhere from three to six months to fill a position through normal channels, and sifting through 200 resumes is labor-intensive, especially if a project suddenly becomes mission critical. Many employers prefer instead to rely on their networks—or their employees' networks—to address a vital need. McGraw-Hill's Brian Jensen explains it this way: "It is a lot about who you know. I don't like to say that, but when I'm looking at John for our job, and John was referred to me by Mary, who I know well, and I know Mary is not going to send me someone who doesn't know what he is doing, it just gives John more credibility."[2]

Stryker Corporation is so keen on employee referrals that it's one of the company's strategic goals. Laurie Byrne, vice president, Global Staffing and Talent Development, said, "We are utilizing our line management and asking them to take more ownership in the process by beginning to network.... It's proven that employee referrals are usually the most successful hires. We know that people have very powerful networks, particularly now."[3]

Part of the reason employee networks are so "powerful" is that on average people work at 12 jobs during their careers—that means they cross paths with hundreds of individuals, maybe thousands, along the way. After spending time with you at a job, they have a good idea about how you work and are in a good position to pass that information along. Newell Rubbermaid's Mike Rickheim said, "We encourage employee referrals because our employees absolutely understand the type of culture and environment that we have and they can help us judge whether the individual would be happy and successful here."[4]

Why is the employer so concerned with your happiness? Besides the fact that happy workers are productive workers, it's also expensive to train you, keep you, and if things don't work out—replace you. Employees are a huge investment—some say the number-one investment—so hiring is serious business. A company's success usually depends on it.

Not to discourage the disconnected, but many career experts claim that approximately 75 percent of all jobs are filled through networking, which leaves millions of people scrambling for the 25 percent of available jobs that are publicly advertised or the ones appearing on the big job boards. We don't have to put those numbers together to convince you that it's much more competitive to vie for those advertised jobs. A better course of action is to—once again—zero in on a few companies that pique your interest and pursue them through your thriving network—or the network you are building today.

How? Remember that 1990 play by John Guare, *Six Degrees of Separation?* One of the premises of the play is that "any two individuals are connected by at most five others." Another name for that is the "human web."[5] We are all connected some way, even if it's a friend of a friend of a friend of a friend of a friend. If you buy into this, and there are plenty of studies validating its truth, the hidden job market starts to become a lot more transparent—and networking doesn't seem quite so daunting. You just have to remember that building a social network takes more time than randomly shooting off your resume into cyberspace.

And that's the rub. Most people who find themselves suddenly unemployed tend to panic. They scour the Internet looking for the immediate opening or spin their wheels going after jobs they are ill-suited for. Try not to do that. Instead think about all the people you know. If you worked hard and treated people fairly in your career, there's a very good chance that others will recommend you—or at least share information with you about companies and positions. Tap into the expertise of your network. People want to share information—as long as it doesn't compromise their primary allegiance. Go into investigative mode. Do your research. Talk to people. Ask for help. Use every opportunity to put the word out that you would like to be considered if a job opens up.

As SAIC's David McMichael said, "I think now more than ever it's important to be network-oriented in your everyday life. The natural connections that you make allow you to connect with a larger peripheral group. And I think those peripheral groups are the folks who can help you get that job interview. In everyday life, I think it's important to exchange business cards with someone who is waiting for a table at the restaurant or someone you are sitting next to on a plane."[6]

But, as we already mentioned, it's much more advantageous if you find your next job before you actually need a new one. That's the position you really want to be in. You need to keep your options open while you still have a job. Unum's Karen Bradbury said, "The most attractive candidate is the candidate who is still working—right or wrong."[7] Hiring managers refer to this as the passive job seeker, although Newell Rubbermaid's Mike Rickheim said, "The term passive job seeker is an interesting one because if you are seeking a job I don't know how passive I actually consider you to be. But, for the purposes of this conversation, let's distinguish between the active, which would be the person who has made a full commitment to look for a new job versus the passive, the one who is willing to entertain some conversations but is not completely focused on it."[8] Actually, Rickheim is right: there's nothing "passive" about someone who is working hard at the old job while staying alert to other prospects. That's proactive.

And that's what you need to be in this fragile job market. Your father may have worked at the same company for 40 years, but that's an anomaly in today's job market. Nowadays there are no guarantees. Instead you have to be on the lookout for your next opportunity. You have to be "poised" to make your next move. According to Pitney Bowes' Laura Terenzi Khaleel, "A poised candidate is somebody who is not actively looking, but if they get the right kind of call, they will consider it. That's another group that we are very interested in as well."[9]

When the 2007 economic meltdown began, many were taken by surprise. People with long-term careers suddenly became just as vulnerable as the newly hired. Certain industries—auto, finance, construction—got trounced. Now that the shellshock has subsided, at least you can be certain of one thing: Don't get too comfortable. The marketplace is undergoing a massive correction—with some industries in retooling mode. Global competition and emerging technology are squeezing the job market so tight that there's no assurance that the job you have today will be around two or three years from now. That's one of the reasons your network is so crucial. The job market is shifting, whether you like it or not, so there's no point in digging in your heels and complaining. Instead, be flexible, be nimble, and reach out. That may mean you may have to do some personal retooling by going back to school for new skills (you may even have to change careers); it definitely means you need to build an extensive network so you are positioned to take advantage of the new opportunities that will present themselves once the shift gains ground.

If networking skills are rusty

If you were gainfully employed for a number of years or even out of the workforce all together, there's a chance that your networking skills may have become rusty. There are a lot of reasons this can happen. Maybe you were so focused on the job in front of you that you forgot about the rest of the world. Or maybe you were at a stage of your life where your growing children took up every extra moment of your time out of work. Or maybe you just shun networks because they seem self-serving. These things happen...but at your own expense.

We need the human web to realize our own potential because nothing happens in a vacuum. Our connections—strong and weak—form a framework for collaboration and strength. If you've allowed your network to lag, it's a good time to rebuild. Your younger colleagues have the right idea. As Abigail Whiffen, the director of Global Recruiting Operations at Unisys, said, "Networking is not a dirty word for this group. I worked at Columbia Business School, from 2001 to 2003, and we were constantly looking for ways to publish, advertise, promote events without using the word *networking*. Now every college student uses the word *networking*, without feeling the need to shy away from it."[10] It is probably no coincidence that this is the generation of college students who embraced social media wholeheartedly—immediately. Social networks gave them a fluid and convenient medium that allowed them to easily connect with friends and colleagues.

But whether you are a newcomer to the workforce or a seasoned pro, it has never been easier to tap into the hidden job market—especially if you employ the tools social media affords. Social networks give you an opportunity to stay on another person's radar almost effortlessly by checking in periodically and updating regularly. To jumpstart your networking, start by making a commitment to set aside some time each day to build and nurture your connections. Check in with your colleagues—past and present. Ask for suggestions and advice. Offer your assistance. Engage in shop talk and find out what's going on in any industry that interests you. As Arthur Houtz, an old friend, used to say, "Always walk and talk." Gather information, share information—it's amazing what you can find out from the most unlikely sources, as long as you are open to the possibilities.

It may take some effort on your part to build a helpful virtual network, but once it is in place, you can expect things to happen fairly quickly. Take, for instance, Olga O'Donnell, a senior manager of monetization at Microsoft. When she was ready to find new employment, O'Donnell sent messages through Facebook and LinkedIn to various connections she had at several key media companies and found a new job within a couple of weeks—beating the average time it takes to find a new job by at least three months. What's important to remember is that O'Donnell's network was alive and well *before* she made a connection with key individuals. She didn't just pop out of the blue and proclaim that she was looking for work.

Networking is all about give and take. CIGNA's Eric Kaulfuss said, "Most people want to be known as altruistic and doing their part to help."[11] Although you may prefer to be known as a giver rather than taker, there are times when you have to ask for help. Do not hesitate to do this. If you have qualms about being on the receiving end, don't worry. Once you are in a better position, you can give help. That's how networking works. Maintain your integrity, give freely, and develop a personal brand, and you'll be back in the swing of things and making inroads into the hidden job market before you know it.

Moving beyond your circle

Fostering an online relationship with people you want to work with in the future should be part of your 2.0 networking campaign. That means you may need to expand beyond your circle of friends— your strong ties—to people who share interests or are friends of friends or industry insiders. In other words, you need to develop some weak ties. According to Wikipedia's definition of a social network,

> Smaller, tighter networks can be less useful to their members than networks with lots of loose connections (weak ties) to individuals outside the main network. More open networks, with many weak ties and social connections, are more likely to introduce new ideas and opportunities to their members than closed networks with many redundant ties. In other

words, a group of friends who only do things with each other already share the same knowledge and opportunities. A group of individuals with connections to other social worlds is likely to have access to a wider range of information.[12]

And those weak ties also don't know about that baseball glove you forgot to return.

Diversifying your network has other benefits, too. It can also lead to broadening your perspective and help you be more receptive to new ideas. You might have thought your skills were relevant only in one field, but, when you talk to another person in a different field, you may find out that these same skills can easily transfer to a different position in another industry. Don't narrow your options, especially when everything is changing so rapidly. Martin Cepeda, senior university recruiter at a Fortune 500 healthcare company, said it's important to recognize the complexity of large companies. Cepeda suggests you use your professional networks and resources to understand "how a company is structured" and/or who it partners with for professional services. Knowing these details can help you tailor your job search based on the type of positions that a company recruits for internally. If a specific function/department is outsourced to a service vendor, this prior knowledge would help direct you on where a job opportunity would exist, for the function that you are looking to work in.[13] This means you may have to drill down deep into your network to find out how an organization is put together. In this case, your weak ties may be more helpful to you than strong ties. That's when you have to get serious about broadening your network.

"Walk and talk," have conversations with distant connections about a particular employer, and never assume that only your strong ties can help you. Everyone has something to offer, so find out what it is. At the end of the day, the more information you have, the more inroads you can make.

This theory of weak ties also relates to another social networking idea: the 1:50 principle, which states that everyone knows at least 50 people and each of those 50 people knows an additional 50 people, so even as your circle widens by degrees of separation, the network becomes large and "weak" (diverse, actually) enough to make things happen. Why is this theory important?

For several reasons, but in essence, job seekers significantly improve their chances of getting hired the wider their networking circle is. Because virtual connections are easier to maintain and foster than traditional networking methods, a job seeker no longer has to wait a month or two for Uncle Joe to introduce his friend at GE and then another month to set up a friendly informational interview. Instead, through a steady development of a strong online presence, job seekers have access to hundreds of possible job leads.

For those who are hesitant about the virtual world because of privacy worries (more about this topic in the next chapter), rest assured that you can avert trouble if you practice discretion. As long as you remember that all your activities are public once you commit to online participation, it is up to you to craft how you are perceived. What's essential is that you don't dismiss social networking entirely before you even understand it. Your technological savvy is an important commodity to employers of the 21st century. Charlotte K. Frank, PhD, a senior vice president of Research and Development at McGraw-Hill, said, "I absolutely expect that new candidates know about social media. We expect people to be knowledgeable about everything happening in the field. They absolutely must feel comfortable working with social media; it is essential to how we do business."[14]

Why employers like LinkedIn

Everyone is at a different stage of engagement in social media. Some of you have hundreds of online connections—a vibrant network that can be tapped in a moment's notice—and some of you have no virtual connections whatsoever. One constant in tapping into the hidden job market, according to the Fortune 500 employers we interviewed, is LinkedIn. For the more advanced, this may seem like a "no brainer," as Electronic Arts's Cindy Nicola called it, but many have not yet jumped on board, even though all the Fortune 500 employers use this platform as a primary sourcing tool.

One of the reasons employers love this platform is because it gives them access to passive candidates. In the days before social media, when Activision's Lissa Freed was in charge of recruiting at Mattel, she said she spent hours and hours researching who worked where.

That's all changed in the Age of LinkedIn. "If you want to find out who's the head of operations at ABC Company, you can search it out through LinkedIn. Or if someone mentions a name, you can go find them there. The top-tier search firms have been challenged by the fact that their databases are compromised now. Those coveted databases that some of these executive search firms had now exist in the open forum."[15] That's a good reason for you to love it as well. If you don't have a connection at your targeted company, you can easily reach out through LinkedIn.

Here's what Ian Decker, director of Talent Acquisition at MetLife, said about LinkedIn:

> Social media has definitely had an impact on hiring at MetLife. The one avenue we have been using for the last four years is LinkedIn. I don't want to say this incorrectly, but I think we were one of LinkedIn's first corporate clients that really started to use LinkedIn to network with candidates and use that portal as an avenue to find and hire talent. LinkedIn has been a tremendous resource for us, both from a networking standpoint to finding candidates. There's also a lot of information and a lot of groups you can join on LinkedIn, which gives you exposure to various blogs and what people are saying about certain industries and what they are saying about certain companies. It's really grown tremendously, and as that has grown, I think our use of social media has grown as well. In the last four years, we have come a long way. The more people who subscribe to LinkedIn, and use it to reach out to their networks and their connections, it's helped employers because the more people that are in it, the more resources we have to find talent.[16]

It's difficult to state exactly how many people are active on LinkedIn because it grows exponentially each day, but as of October 2010, there were 80 million members.[17] If you consider that approximately 80 million Americans work full time, LinkedIn's numbers are impressive. And numbers matter in social media, so if you have a professional niche site, that's well and good, but as far as sourcing goes, LinkedIn should supplement your other platform.

LinkedIn numbers include members from more than 200 countries. Lisa Whittington, a vice president of Human Resources at Host Hotels & Resorts, said, "I'm just starting to look into the 2.0 job market. I opened an international position, which I thought was really interesting, in Amsterdam, and that's how we found the candidate, through LinkedIn. It was amazing and it was fast and it was inexpensive."[18] Lisa Whittington upgraded her LinkedIn account from personal to business with a small investment, but companies can purchase even more access and be privy to LinkedIn's entire database. Ron Gosdeck, a vice president of Global Recruiting at Unisys, said:

> Eighteen months ago, we didn't know what social media was, so we started getting into it by looking at multiple options, including Facebook, Twitter, and LinkedIn. From a recruiting perspective for us, I think LinkedIn is probably the most significant advance because we purchased access to every resume in the database from LinkedIn, so we can search anybody who's in there. We've had significant success in signing very high profile, high level individuals via LinkedIn that we've recruited internally, which means for us that we don't go outside and spend money on a third-party search firm.[19]

If you are looking for a job, you want to be found, so, at the very least, LinkedIn is a necessary tool. Proceed carefully and ask for help if social media is new to you. At Avnet, Claudia Reilly was thinking of setting up "a reverse mentoring program," so individuals who were not comfortable in social media could reach out to younger colleagues for assistance. She said, "You know, all companies do mentoring. What about reverse mentoring? How would the most recent generation view what the baby boomers are looking at? Totally different. I would start with a LinkedIn immersion and then decide how it works best for me and try to understand it."[20] CSC's Jim Gattuso added that setting up an account on LinkedIn is a three-step process: "One is to do some research.... Two is to ask someone who may be more comfortable with social media as a platform and tell that person you want to get out there. Ask for some help in getting set up.... And I think the third thing is that once you have those things established, don't be afraid to start slow. Just remember that everything you put out there has the potential of being publicly available."[21]

Building a robust profile in LinkedIn

Getting started on LinkedIn is simple. Go to *www.linkedin.com* and set up an account. It's free, but you can also purchase premium products—which are recommended for people using the site for professional purposes (sales, recruitment)—for a monthly fee, starting at $24.95. If you take a more "passive" approach and you just want to be found by an employer, then you can set up a profile and join groups through the free, basic service. The subscription service could be overwhelming until you have a good grasp of the basics, so, as Jim Gattuso advised, start slow, unless you are a recruiter or need to investigate and drill down more deeply into the layers of a corporation.

Start by providing your name and profession. Upload your current resume—the one you just revamped with your personal brand in mind. Spelling errors will not enhance your personal brand, so make sure you are careful and clear when you input this information. Do not forget about the importance of keywords, and, if you have a very specific title that may not be recognizable outside your company, use more generic keywords. Be as diligent when crafting your profile in LinkedIn as you would be if you were writing your resume.

LinkedIn will show you how to build your network by asking for access to your e-mail account. You will have to feel comfortable giving your password information to a trusted third party, but, if you do provide this information, LinkedIn will make the connections between your e-mail account and its members. With your permission, it goes through your e-mail address book and then allows you to see your connections network so that you can build your network and invite your contacts to connect (they have to be members of LinkedIn, too). You may also add additional people manually into your network.

After you have registered, create a profile. Remember this is *your brand* you are creating—at least your professional brand—so keep these guidelines in mind:

1. Add a photo. Remember, LinkedIn is a professional site, so the photo should be one that you would use for business purposes. Keep your family photos on Facebook. Kathy Hooson, a recruiter for Hewlett-Packard, said, "Candidates

should remember that all information added to their profile on LinkedIn might be taken into consideration during the selection process, so they need to be accurate and professional in their approach, including the photo that might be displayed. I have found conflicts in important information when reviewing."[22]

2. Fill out the profile so that it is complete, and make sure there are no typos. Again, your profile represents your Digital Self, your professional self, your brand. Use keywords, even in your profile, to describe yourself. Ryder's Kirk Imhof said, "From a skill-set perspective, when doing searches on LinkedIn, having very specific titles can work to your benefit or your detriment. If your primary job duty of your role is not in your title, it's going to be very hard for a recruiter to find you if they're doing a resume or profile search by a very specific job title. So what would be helpful is using the true level of your position. Whether it's a manager, whether it's a director, whether it's an officer, like a VP, the level of the position would be appropriate because it allows the recruiter to hone in on a targeted experience level. As for the job title, if you're really not looking to attract a lot of opportunities, use a very specific job title to narrow down the amount of recruitment that comes your way. Otherwise, general titles may gain you additional attention—though the role may not fit your specific experience. A good example would be a title such as Sales Manager vs. Call Center Manager. Both deal with sales, but only the Call Center Manager job title indicates to the recruiter your specific sales leadership experience."[23]

3. Sections of the profile, such as education and prior companies you worked for, are more important than others because they allow you to tap into your network. Avnet's Claudia Reilly said, "I would start with not only going into LinkedIn to a person in the area of business that I wanted to go into, but I also think I would focus on something in their profile that connected us, be it, we went to the same college, we have the same interest in some charity we work with. Something that would spark a connection personally, like, "Hey, you went to USC; so did I."[24]

4. Visit the Public Profile Settings—your privacy settings—so you can control what people see. MediaLink's Chris Nutile said, "I think people need to keep LinkedIn up to date.... There are a lot of privacy opportunities within LinkedIn, just like any of the other social networking tools. If you don't want people to see your network (many recruiters spend years building up a strong network on LinkedIn, and because most of those people might be candidates, they may not want other recruiters to have access to it by just clicking on their name and looking through their contact list), you can hide that; you can say, 'No, I don't want this to be seen by people.' There are all sorts of opportunities for privacy baked into all the social networks. Privacy will be more and more of an issue as we move forward."[25]

5. Finally, join groups! This is a good opportunity to display your expertise. When you engage with other like minds, you get an opportunity to talk about the things you enjoy about your profession. It can add cement to what interests you about your work and it can help you also tap into the hidden job market. You can build up the language of your profession, too, if it doesn't come naturally to you. But keep in mind that less is often more. Be concise and don't scatter your efforts far and wide. Pitney Bowes' Laura Terenzi Khaleel said, "I think if I see that somebody belongs to 10 different groups, that's not necessarily going to make me say, 'Oh wow, that's a great candidate.' It might simply mean that they spend a lot of time networking via LinkedIn. However, the types of groups they belong to, if we're looking for a particular type of engineer or a particular type of software developer, and they belong to associations specific to that skill set, that's going to hold weight with us. That means they are keeping up with the technology and they're staying current and they know a lot of other folks."[26] In the event you connect with someone who is working at your targeted company, build a relationship with that person in your group while you discuss the latest industry news. Engage. But as Kellogg's Carolyn Rice

said, "I was very careful not to ask for anything. I did not want to create an obligation. You don't want people to feel responsible for you in any way, so I asked questions about positions without asking the person to do anything for me directly. I'm not sure what you would call this psychologically, but it's better to position yourself so that you do not look desperate."[27]

A full picture

LinkedIn will let you know how much of your profile is completed as you move along. It's a good idea to create a full-bodied picture—with recommendations from former colleagues or supervisors—as well as uploading your resume, if you are serious about finding a new position. But remember too much information can do as much harm as too little information. No one has time to wade through "chapter and verse" particulars. Always be concise in your job-hunting approach. Paul Marchand, a vice president of Global Talent Acquisition at PepsiCo, said, "I have seen people do a really nice job of LinkedIn profiles. But as a leader of talent acquisition and a person who has been doing recruiting for 20 years on and off on different assignments, I do think that some of the same rules apply in a traditional paper resume as they should apply online. What I mean by that is, the best LinkedIn resumes are crisp, tight bullet points, you know, give me the headlines, give me the sound bites, let me quickly review it and walk away with the elevator 5-second speech."[28]

Once you have completed your profile and it's in excellent shape, connect with your network—extend your reach far and wide. Zero in on your targeted companies and start a conversation. Start with the hiring managers or recruiters and introduce yourself. CIGNA's Eric Kaulfuss suggests, "If you go to a company Website or a job posting site, and you have this LinkedIn bar up there, it will tell you who you know or who's in your network at this company. My thought is that you zero in on the HR people, especially the recruiters, having applied as well, and say, 'Hey, I just want you to know I applied to this job. I'm connected to you through LinkedIn, if you wouldn't mind introducing me to whomever the recruiter is.' I found that to be a very effective approach. It shows some initiative. It shows some research. It shows some judgment. And those are the types of things we are looking for when we hire people anyway. We want them to take initiative. We want them to have good judgment. We want them to be polite. So that type of thing leads to, 'Okay, this person sounds great.' And it also gives you a chance to look at their background if they are qualified or not as you're looking at that introduction. Most people do like to do those introductions in LinkedIn. That's probably why it works. I think people like you to know that they know people and they're connected."[29]

Plan to periodically revisit your LinkedIn profile to refresh and update—and, certainly, link to others with whom you share a common bond or interest. If you go to a career fair, ask the recruiter if you can link with them—as soon as possible. Even if they don't have a position at that moment, at the very least you have made a preliminary connection. Build on it.

We asked Shally Steckerl for a few suggestions on how to hone your investigative skills when looking for a job. Steckerl is an executive vice president at Arbita and is the founder and Chief CyberSleuth of JobMachine, Inc. (jobmachine.net), the premier provider of sourcing consulting services and workforce development. Early in his career Steckerl realized that as a contingency recruiter he could beat the competition by finding people who were not available in mainstream sources. Since then he has been instrumental in building numerous world-class sourcing and research organizations. Because of his passion for the Internet as a recruitment tool and his continually innovative methods, Steckerl has developed a reputation as one of the most respected authorities in passive candidate research and talent pipeline development worldwide. A pioneer in recruitment Internet research, accomplished author and celebrated speaker, he is a regular contributor to many industry publications. Steckerl currently consults with organizations interested in building passive candidate pipeline generation and recruitment teams and developing their advanced sourcing skills.

What job search engine includes only jobs from companies' own employment pages and not from job boards?

GetTheJob does this, as does DirectEmployers.com for its 300-plus member companies. To maximize reach and efficiency, most employers don't list a job solely on their Websites. Many employer jobs are cross-posted on various boards (our parent company pioneered the technology to automate this in the early 1990s), so it may appear a job comes from a board, even when the employer's site is the source. To see the most job postings, you are currently best off with job aggregator sites, such as Indeed.com, SimplyHired.com, Juju.com. Remember, when your search results appear, you can set an e-mail alert or RSS feed to keep getting relevant results.

Will Google and its fellow Web crawlers plan to spider actual companies' employment pages?

First, there are technical hurdles to index dynamically generated content (bots currently can't do that well), which is unfortunately the platform for most job databases. This caused Google to go in another direction for now: Get companies and job boards to facilitate it. Google base lets people upload jobs and submit other kinds of content free, which also end up in regular Google search results. And most job meta-aggregators have figured out how to make the jobs they collect appear in search engine results. We don't know their plans, but if one can make money from spidering any kind of online content, it's just a matter of time.

How do you get phone numbers or e-mail addresses for people you find?

For phone numbers, you can call the company's main number (listed on its Website) and ask to be transferred to [Name]. Try Argali.com (free download) or Zabasearch.com for home phones. For phone or e-mail, check their social network profiles (Wink lets you find most all of them), which often list contact information. Otherwise, for e-mails, the Webinar presentation mentioned the search engine method, i.e., typing "Firstname Lastname" (CompanyName OR *@companyemaildomain), but you can also try typing author:@oracle.com at Google Groups (substitute the company email domain of your desired person) and click on any message in your results. Then click View Profile next to the message author's name. This will reveal the e-mail format for the company. Most of the time it's first initial plus last name @, firstname.lastname@ or firstname_lastname@ so you could just e-mail all three and whichever doesn't bounce back is the right one!

When looking for a job on a search engine, how should I choose which item goes first in the search query?

Start with most important keywords first, then least important at the end of the string. When searching for potential hiring managers, start with company name(s), then job title(s), then any unique skill terms/jargon, and end with geographic filters (area codes and state abbreviation).

What if you know a person's name and phone, but not what company they work for?

Try a reverse phone lookup with Argali (free download) or simply type the person's name on an aggregated search tool like Wink.com that searches profiles across most major social networks. Or simply type the person's name (inside quotation marks) on a regular search engine.

How can I gather the e-mail addresses of my Facebook friends, so I can conduct a mailing to them?

You currently can't export friends' contact information from Facebook. But you can search Facebook and then use the person and company name with the above-mentioned method to get their e-mail and/or phone.

Social networks let me target people searches geographically, but how can I find people in my field in my local area, who may not be on those networks?

You could search membership rosters or post networking messages within local chapters of relevant associations, user groups, etc. Find their resumes or bios via search engines (add geographic criteria to your searches, such as area code/state). Google also allows zip code range search.

How can I find out about what people in my Facebook or Twitter universe works at a given company?

Posting "Tom is looking for someone who can introduce him to the right manager at X company" seems inefficient and whiny. What works better? On Facebook, type the company name in the main search (top right box on homepage), click the People tab in your results, then after Show Results From, select My Networks in the menu (though you'd have more results with the default All Networks). A tool that lets you search through friends' bios only for keywords, locations, etc., is TweepSearch (click Help for how-to) but again, you might want to use Twitter itself to search through everyone.

When building a social network, should I focus on people who know me well for my first-degree connections?

No. If you worked at the same company with someone but not with them, maybe bumped into each other occasionally, they should be made first-degree connections. Same for people you went to school with, and maybe had a class in common. You don't have to be buddies with someone to make them first degree. They have something in common (membership in an association, etc.). First degree should extend to them as well.

When building a social network (on LinkedIn), should my emphasis be to add as many well-connected people as possible, even though I hardly know them and they know nothing about me?

Yes and no. It's fine to add the super-connectors who accept connections from anyone (these so-called Open Networkers are people who have an icon of a ring of small blue circles next to their name and/or display their e-mail address on their profiles). You can find these people in many ways, such as at TopLinked.com. If you want to add people in your particular industry, then first reach out with a short get-to-know-you communication (not a connection request).

Is professional credibility or having something substantive in common crucial when asking for introductions?

Having worked at the same company, attended the same school, being members of the same association, or having any other common interest is sufficient to initiate an introduction. But if you want to be introduced to someone, choose the person who you think knows you best, would be more likely to do you a favor, and/or would give the most meaningful introduction. LinkedIn lets you pick the person among those with a path to your target to forward the introduction through.

After using LinkedIn's Outlook contacts import, it shows hundreds of names of my contacts using LinkedIn. Should I send a mass invitation through LinkedIn to connect?

No, because if some of those contacts are old and the recipient clicks the "I don't know this person" button on the connection request, you get a strike against you. Certain restrictions on your account begin after five strikes. This can be remedied, but it's safer to send a mass e-mail via regular e-mail with a link to your profile, requesting they click it and connect or give their permission for you to make the connection.

Filtering for LinkedIn Open Networkers when searching. Open Networkers are great contacts to have when you are looking for a job because they are individuals who are willing to accept connections from people they don't yet know, and they will likely be able to introduce you to other key influencers, even if they themselves are not in a position to further your job search. On the Advanced Search form, search only open network members (the checkbox beside the circle of colored blue and orange dots).

Once you find someone via social networks that you want to approach for a job, is it best to just send a direct message and see if they will talk with you?

Yes, but first try to learn something about the person by looking at their profiles, their past blogposts, etc., much as you would prefer to research your recipient when sending a resume so the cover letter isn't generic. How you approach matters: Be succinct, think about what would intrigue the recipient, and lead with that. Don't indicate a job-hunting need in the first communication. Focus on how you can help them (not your job-search), a common point of interest (same industry niche, location, alma mater, etc.) and just a Web link leading to more detail about you.

How do I create a group on LinkedIn?

Go to LinkedIn Groups Directory search and see if another similar group exists. (If another such group is large and active, you may or may not want to create your own.) Click the Create a Group button and follow the free steps. For step-by-step, see LinkedIn's blogpost on it.

Why create a group on LinkedIn when I'm just looking for work?

First, having your own group, it allows you to see the contact details of everyone who asks to join your group, so you could save that contact information for future outreach. Second, you can help shape the group's focus by inviting people in your area of interest. As the group grows, you create a network that helps you both to find work and to enhance your career and others' even afterwards. You create goodwill that pays you back in unforeseen ways.

What is the most important factor to the success of a group on LinkedIn?

The level of participation. If it's not seeded with posts early on, and builds in activity, it will wither and die. So don't just get people to join. Encourage them to post news, updates, jobs, respond to discussions, etc.[30]

Chapter 4

A Thousand In-Laws From Boston

Even with privacy filters and controls, assume that if it is on the Internet it is fair game.
—Cindy Nicola
Vice President of Global Talent Acquisition
Electronic Arts

Let's compare social media to a big Thanksgiving dinner. All the parents, grandparents, children, aunts, uncles, and cousins are gathered around the table. With all that food around, everyone is feeling good, chattering away, so you decide to add your two cents to the conversation. Film buff that you are, you start critiquing *Wall Street: Money Never Sleeps.* Everyone smiles as you yap away, even when you slip and call Michael Douglas "Kirk." It's all good, even the Kirk part. Your relatives are so distracted by the noxious brussels sprouts that no one notices your gaffe, except your surly in-law from Boston.

When social media first came upon the scene, you may have treated it—with all the conversations, all the distractions, all the excitement—as a one-big-happy-family experience. That's understandable. Social media encourages engaging with as many connections as remotely possible.

That's part of the fun. What's not so fun is that you may have ignored another important facet of social media; namely: that it's all public information. Along with all your new friends and family, you may now have hundreds (thousands or millions) of new in-laws from Boston—and one of them could turn out to be a hiring manager at the company you just sent your resume to.

We all do dumb things. We all say dumb things. We can admit this—to our nearest and dearest—because we know it's human to make mistakes. But now we have this powerful technology to remind us—and everyone else who cares to know—just how dumb we can be. That's the reality of not practicing digital restraint.

By now, most of us have heard the horror stories—the lost jobs, the lost degrees, the lost friendships, the lost loves—that result from digital recklessness. Still, many of us go into denial (maybe because sitting in front of a computer late at night feels more private than public) about what's "fair game" on the Internet. It's not surprising that the issue of privacy is such a hot debate these days; we persistently want to believe that we have control over the information we share digitally. Well, we don't have control, even with privacy settings—at least not yet.

Chris Nutile, director, MediaLink Executive Search, spoke to us about a hiring decision he made while he was working for Yahoo!. He said:

> We were ready to extend an offer. We had done the references, we were ready to go. At the last minute, I was looking at the candidate's resume and he had his blog on it. I hadn't looked at it before, so I took 5 minutes to read the blog out of curiosity. It was well written, insightful, and engaging. Then I got to a part of the blog where the person was talking about how much he hated the people in his office, how much he hated his job, and how he would like to kill this one person he worked with. Right away, I said, "We cannot move forward with this candidate and I contacted the candidate. I always feel as a recruiter that it is best to be open and share to see if you can help somebody." I just said, "Unfortunately, I can't extend the offer to you." The candidate was shocked, and said, "Why? Everything seemed to be going well with the process. I don't understand." I said, "Well, I read your blog

and I came across the entry about wanting to kill someone in your office." The candidate said, "You had no right to read my blog!" I said, "It's public information. I could have gotten your blog off any search engine." But I said, "On top of that, you listed it on your resume, which really opens the door for me to read it." He said, "Well you don't think I was serious and that I actually wanted to kill someone?" I said, "No, I don't believe you're going to do any physical harm, but the fact is that you talked about how you hated your job, how you hated the people you work with, and to say that you wanted to kill someone and put it out there in public shows me a great deal of foolishness by not understanding the digital space and the digital world that we live in. Also, Yahoo! has a legal responsibility to provide a safe workplace for our employees."[1]

Understanding the digital space means that once your online words are released into the cloud that information is accessible to the public—or, at least, anyone who has access to a computer. It also means your inglorious self can hang out in the digital stratosphere for a very long time. Why? Because the statute of limitations regarding dumb pronouncements on the Web doesn't apply. Add to this the fact that human beings have a penchant for the negative—good news is just not as interesting—and the "permanent memory bank of the Web increasingly means there are no second chances."[2]

Was it ever thus?

Innovations in communication often generate heated debates about privacy. Judge Wesley Brown, the oldest federal judge still hearing cases, remembers the early days of the telephone when "You'd call a central operator...and she knew about what everybody was doing all over the community."[3] The Wichita, Kansas judge thinks all the fuss about privacy is easily resolved—as long as you make a decision to live a life without secrets. A nice idea, but let's face it, the judge is 103 years old, so his wild oats have been oatmeal for a while. As much as we may appreciate transparency and a forthright approach, it's not quite as simple when you're in your stormy teens or 20s.

And remember the early days of e-mail? We were warned: "Write an e-mail as though it could end up on the front page of the *New York Times*."[4] That was a surprise, learning a company had access to an individual's business e-mail. Most of us made adjustments. We stopped forwarding off-color jokes or sending gripes about the boss to our colleague in the cubicle across the room. We didn't really have a choice; our livelihood was at stake. But, regardless of the consequences, some people ignored them. In fact, to this day, there are individuals who—company policy be damned—get fired because they refuse to believe the rules about e-mail apply to them.

So all this transparency has been a slippery slope for many people—especially if you are younger—but, if it's any consolation, it's also been an issue for some Fortune 500 companies. Many employers have ambivalence deciding exactly what information is "fair game" and what is not. Avnet's Claudia Reilly said, "We don't go out to view the Facebook and MySpace pages of candidates, unless we are invited. That's their privacy. That's what their personal life is. And I'm not going to base my decision on it. We do background checks. We do legal background checks set by our legal department and leadership of what we're going to check—besides the skill set and education."[5]

This position was echoed by other Fortune 500 employers. Unum's Karen Bradbury said, "We don't look at social networks or Google candidates as part of the hiring process.... A company has to be extremely careful about anything like that because doing an Internet search or Googling someone is not necessarily a very reliable way of getting accurate information on people. What we really rely on is the background checks that we do on folks."[6]

CSC's Jim Gattuso concurs. In certain hires, his company Googles a prospective candidate—after thoroughly vetting them—because

> Reviewing the information that is available about a person in the public domain can be something we would want to check. It isn't something that we have to do or have a mandate to do, but, particularly at the management level, I think you want to understand the folks who are going to be representing your team from a management or executive capacity, then do your due diligence to be sure there's nothing in that person's

background that could at some point become embarrassing or harmful to us as an employer. If something is raised, we will certainly go back to that person and discuss it with them, just to be sure all the facts are right. We would go back because in fairness not everything that's out there on Google is true. Candidates deserve a platform and we need to give them the chance to address any issues.[7]

The glow of Google

Google searches do indeed turn up faulty information. As part of our research, we did a Google search on our names. Brenda Greene found a quotation attributed to her about a restaurant, "Citron 47," an establishment she has never visited. It was not particularly damaging information—just untrue, so she sent an e-mail to the Websites that displayed this quotation to ask that it be removed. Tracking down the various Websites and writing e-mails to individual Webmasters (if no other way to contact the site was provided) was time-consuming. If the material had serious implications, she could have hired a company to eradicate the false information (or at least bury it), but it would have been at her expense—and online reputation management can be costly.

We heard about a particularly troublesome case a few months back. Jane Doe (not her real name) was diagnosed with an illness and given prescription drugs. She eventually became addicted to these prescription drugs and started buying them illegally. On one occasion, she bought a lot of pills at a bulk price. She got caught—and then she got implicated as a player in a drug ring. She got arrested. Having been a former community leader, her name appeared in a few newspapers. She lost her job. So far, so bad.

Jane made a decision to go to rehab. She cleaned up her act, appeared in court and proved her innocence as far as the drug ring. The felony was dismissed, although she was charged with a misdemeanor. Phew. Her life had finally turned around, so she decided to apply for a new job. She was experienced and successful prior to her wrong turn. She sent her resume out. Although the recession was in full bloom, she immediately got a call to come in for an interview. The interview went extremely well. She did not get the job. She discovered that the company had Googled her, and the prospective employer had read the newspaper articles. She tried to explain her situation, but the employer had already hired someone else. Jane sent out a few more resumes. Nothing happened, so she sent out a few more. What she didn't realize is that each time she sent a resume out and an employer checked her out through Google, those old newspaper articles about her felony arrest moved up in page rank. When she wasn't looking for a job, those articles were buried a few pages back in Google, but once employers hit them, up they rose. As far as those employers were concerned, Jane had committed a felony—she had been involved in a drug ring! The rest of her story didn't matter at that point.

This may seem like an extreme case, but it points to the current transparency—whether you are actively living your life online or not. Jane Doe did not engage in social networking, yet she still felt the ramifications of Internet exposure.

The glow of Google can be troubling because Google relies on an algorithm to determine what's important—page rank (the first page listings are those that get the most hits). Most users don't scroll beyond the first page, so that's why search engine optimization is so fashionable right now; everyone wants the first page—except Jane Doe or people in a similar predicament. Rank can be manipulated by SEO experts and spammers, so some people are veering away from the big three search engines—Google, Yahoo!, and Bing—and instead tapping into search engines that don't rely solely on an algorithm but actually have human beings (and their slashtags) determining whether the information is from a trustworthy site. Blekko is one such upstart.

But even if Blekko suddenly became the search engine of choice—a definite long shot—it still wouldn't help Jane Doe. The information about her felony appeared in legitimate sources, so Jane needs to go to the newspapers and ask that this information be removed (although it is doubtful the newspapers would remove it from their archives). Then, after contacting the newspapers, she can, according to Shally Steckerl, executive vice president at Arbita, a recruitment solutions firm, petition Google to remove information. (Go to Google's Webmaster Central, then go to the Help Center, and click on the bar that reads

"Need to remove content from Google search results? Here's how.")

This could be a lot of work for someone not particularly adept in navigating the Web.

The lesson is, now more than ever, you need to protect your reputation. A bad decision on your part can have a very long shelf life, so try to be more deliberate—instead of unthinking—about sharing information online with people you do not know. You never know how something you say may be misconstrued or taken out of context or twisted beyond recognition. Not everyone has good intentions.

All of the Fortune 500 employers we spoke to for *The Web 2.0 Job Finder* have a thorough vetting process, but some employers still relied on Google, especially in the initial stages of recruitment. Their attitude was that if the information is online—whether it is a blog, a comment, a complaint, even a photograph or a video—then they have every right and a responsibility to view it. You allow access, whether you realize it or not, simply by putting it out there—and you may unknowingly disqualify yourself from a position by putting out the wrong material. That's why it's essential, as Chris Nutile said earlier, to "understand the digital space and how it affects your professional brand."

People who blend the personal with the professional on social networks certainly are more prone to error than those who compartmentalize their information by using privacy screens and restrictions. Call it a byproduct of youthful fervor, but wearing the heart on the sleeve can have serious consequences. UPS's Matt Lavery said, "Kids think it's a conversation between friends or a group of friends. They forget that it's out there for everyone to see. What they forget is that if it's a private conversation, you probably shouldn't have it [digitally]."[8] While Jim Gattuso, Computer Science Corporation's director of Staffing, agrees with Lavery, he also mentioned that some younger people handle this blend well: "I have a daughter who just graduated from college, and while I make a great distinction between my LinkedIn account, which I consider a professional platform, and my Facebook account, which I consider a personal, more friends and family platform, her view of Facebook is much more of a blended view where she networks with people; she asks people within her professional circle questions and that is a blended platform, which combines both personal and professional. I think blended platforms are going to grow."[9] As this younger generation grows up, blending personal and professional will probably become the norm rather than the exception, so employers and job seekers will have to meet halfway.

In many respects, this generation is not really any different from preceding generations. Dan McMackin, from UPS, said, "When I got hired, the company could never find that stuff out about you."[10] The Web changed everything. Now it's shining a light on activities that just your closest friends were privy to, so it's important to remember to practice digital discretion. We are not yet comfortable with open books. As Cindy Nicola, a VP of global talent acquisition at Electronic Arts, said, "Use common sense with how you present yourself in any online community, even if they are separate. You never know when a friend becomes a colleague or a colleague becomes a friend."[11]

Change the tune

Instead of using the Web as a venting mechanism—full of your heartaches, complaints, and unruly outings—start engaging on more substantial levels. Talk about your passions and share your vision. Develop a brand. If you don't know precisely what your passion or brand is, you may actually discover it as you think and write about it—and end up manifesting it in the process. Use the digital landscape to further your cause.

If you've already made a mess of things digitally, don't despair. These things happen when innovation occurs. Repair the damage and move on. When Facebook's Zuckerberg made a mistake, "blogging venture capitalist Rick Segal begged us to give Zuckerberg some slack. 'He is going to make lots of mistakes, and he will continue to learn and grow.... We need to use care in beating up Zuckerberg and Facebook in general because we want these folks to push the limits of finding new ideas and trying to make sense out of all the data flowing everywhere."[12] The same goes for others who are pushing the medium—and stretching sensibilities.

Social networks are growing up, but they certainly have not yet matured. The kinks are still being ironed out. Experimentation is still vital. In the future, data may have an expiration date and privacy controls may become bullet-proof. Until that happens, though, we need to revisit our own attitudes regarding access to all this information. Young social networkers have indeed made mistakes, but we are all learning from them, so it wouldn't be a bad idea if employers cut them some slack. Some do and some don't, but, in this case, we have to acknowledge the kids have done some heavy lifting.

So with all this hoopla about the pitfalls of social media (which this book may have even contributed to with its own cautionary tales), we want to be clear about our position: Social networking's advantages far outweigh the disadvantages. Social media strengthens collaboration. It allows for quick access to information. Weak ties become strong ties with networks growing exponentially. We are able to maintain a larger network and keep in touch with connections that historically may have been lost. It creates a robust exchange of ideas. Social networks have the potential to nudge a parochial point of view into a more worldly perspective. It allows individuals to build their own brand. It allows interested parties to take the pulse of current trends. And let's not forget that social networking is entertaining as well—allowing you to easily keep in touch with friends and family who may have moved a distance, psychically or geographically. Although it's true there are some drawbacks, which we reiterated in this chapter, if the older generation wants to stay current and knowledgeable about the changing marketplace, it would be wise to keep an open mind and engage in social media. Just rely on your finely honed discretionary skills, and you'll be fine, especially if you ask your younger cohorts for some advice.

Background checks

Sometimes job seekers operate on faulty assumptions. They inflate their resumes, they neglect to include or conveniently hide an employment mishap during a job interview, thinking no one will ever notice the difference. We recommended in the chapter about resumes that you practice honesty. It's the best policy—for a whole lot of reasons. But, just in case you had any misgivings, you need to know that large companies do thorough background checks before they hire. Ron Gosdeck, vice president of Global Recruiting at Unisys, said, "In our case, everybody in the U.S. who gets hired gets a background check. They either meet the standard that's been set or they don't."[13]

Even prior to Web 2.0, the individual was pretty transparent. In fact, a lot of detailed information has been available for decades. Typically, according to the Privacy Rights Clearinghouse, a background check nowadays may cover the following: Driving records, vehicle registration, credit records, criminal records, Social Security number, education records, court records, workers' compensation, bankruptcy, character references, neighbor interviews, medical records, property ownership, military records, state licensing records, drug test records, past employers, personal references, incarceration records, sex offender lists.[14] Certainly background checks vary in degree, but you can rest assured that the big stuff will turn up. Pitney Bowes' Laura Terenzi Khaleel said, "Every single hire at our company has to successfully complete our background check and our drug screening before they can set foot into our doors as an employee. The more senior level the hire, the more traditional reference checks we do, where we are actually picking up the phone and asking for a reference."[15]

This may cause you to feel uncomfortable, but background checks that large companies engage in—along with their other screening processes—can actually work in your favor.[16] Smaller businesses (which employ more than 65 percent of the working population) do not always vet a candidate as thoroughly. Background checks are costly, so many of these companies rely solely on the Internet to initially screen applicants. That could spell trouble for many job seekers, especially for those who have been somewhat reckless.[17]

Before applying for a new position, then, you should Google your name. Clear up any faulty information. Repair any damage you can. Make sure, if there is compromising information on Facebook or other social networks, that privacy settings are in place. Way before the last round in a job interview in which you are seriously considered for a position, you should check and make sure all your offline records are accurate and sound as well. A lot of factors go into a hiring decision, some of which you have no control over. Be a professional about the things you can monitor. And be vigilant, always, where your reputation is concerned.

Chapter 5

What's My Social Strategy?

The Internet isn't written in pencil.
—Erica Albright character
The Social Network

Your social strategy should enhance the perception your friends, family, colleagues, and even strangers have about you. Whether it is information you are posting, snippets about your daily life, or information others are posting about you, this information is all being absorbed by other people, who will in turn form an opinion one way or the other about you. People who don't know you—strangers—will draw assumptions about you based on the information they find or just happen to see. It's essential that you remember, according to Kellogg's Carolyn Rice, that you are "the author of this experience."[1]

By going to major search engines (Google, Bing, Zoom Info) or social networking sites (Facebook, MySpace, LinkedIn, Twitter), in a few minutes interested parties can gather information and find out what you are all about. We hope it's not a scary thought.

As we mentioned in Chapter 4, as part of our research, we Googled ourselves. When Coleen Byrne did a search, she found links to her Facebook page, her likes and dislikes, television shows she watched, a link to her LinkedIn account, photos of her wedding and children, her participation as an adviser at Open Colony, and information about the upcoming book, *The Web 2.0 Job Finder.* From the information on Coleen, strangers may infer she is a professional, is married, is a mother, is an avid networker, knows the Internet space, likes comedy sitcoms, and she may own a Prius (as it is one of her likes on Facebook).

Always ask, Does it hurt or help?

When so much information is available, you need to think about the perception an individual will develop when reading it. If all your social postings have typos and misspellings, people may think you don't have strong written communication skills or that you don't pay attention to detail or you are just plain lazy and careless. If all of your photos show you traveling the world, they may deduce you have a global perspective or you are fluent in language and culture. If people read your blog and it is about how unhappy you are with your work situation, people may assume you have low morale—or you're ready to make a move to a new job. If your daily Facebook posts talk about your yoga classes and workshops, and people in your network are readily engaging in what you are saying about yoga, you may be perceived as a resource on this topic. If you are tweeting information about your industry, people may follow you on Twitter and consider you a possible job lead or industry insider. Most information on the Internet is public information, so ask yourself, "What information am I posting online? Where am I posting that information? What are my friends posting about me? How does this information help my digital image? How does this information hurt my digital image?"

To some extent we can control what appears online about us. Taking some time to think about these factors will help you determine what your digital strategy is and the approach you need to take in the digital world. As SAIC's David McMichael said, "Social media is essentially forcing people to be conscious of their own personal brand."[2]

Because we are putting so much information about ourselves online, allowing people to access information about our lives, and giving them information that basically enables them to make a first impression without even knowing us, it is important to take a step back and think about how we control the message that is being sent out about us and make sure it is consistent with who we are and how we want people to perceive us. Because much of the information out there on the Web can be controlled by you, think about crafting an online brand that flatters your core competencies or enhances others' perception of you. Ask yourself the following three questions:

1. What's your digital brand?
2. Who is your audience?
3. Which sites will nurture your online presence best?

We asked all of our Fortune 500 participants if they Google a prospective candidate. Some say they did, some say they didn't, and some say they have a company policy against it, but they weren't sure what others in the company did when they were vetting a prospective employee. MetLife's Ian Decker readily admitted to Googling a candidate. He said, "I think Googling somebody, you can get some good information. It depends on how much people make public about themselves. Are they on Facebook? Are they tweeting? What are they saying about themselves? And what are they saying they did this weekend? You can tell a lot about people by what they are saying about themselves—unfortunately or fortunately."[3]

Why do I need a social strategy?

Having a strategy—or at least a short-term plan—about how you are going to get where you want to go is essential nowadays. You don't hop in a car and assume you'll find the store you've never been to—without directions. You don't pull out the flour and bake a cake—without a recipe. You don't pull your car's transmission to pieces—without a manual. You could do all these things without instructions, but most of us would end up making a mess without some good orderly direction, so have a plan when you venture into the digital space. And the plan should help you rather than hurt you. Let your better self guide you, so whether you are a good corporate citizen or an unruly maverick, be true to who you are, but be sure you're also coming across as a decent human being. In his book *Socialnomics*, Erik Qualman reminds us, "Social media rewards first-class behavior and punishes improper behavior (What happens in Vegas stays on YouTube)."[4]

So maybe there was that one New Year's party where you had one too many drinks and your friend thought it would be hilarious to post those photos online. Fast forward: Recruiter A, who doesn't know you from Adam, sees the photos and says, "This guy needs a program." Or maybe you are having a bad day and you rant on your blog about how utterly impossible one of your coworkers is. Recruiter B, who again doesn't know you, assumes you are an insufferable snob or miserable at work—and the slanderous information about your coworker doesn't go over too well either. These influencers might not project the true you, but someone who doesn't know you doesn't know that. What strangers do know is that the information is out there, and either all of the above is true or you don't understand the digital space. Neither enhances your image, so when decision time rolls around, the other four candidates who didn't have information on the Web that raised a red flag get the call instead of you—regardless of your stellar qualifications. "Your social brand personalizes you and could be what provides the difference that gets you the job,"[5] Vincent Taguiped, a recruitment manager, said.

When you are putting your resume on LinkedIn, creating a Facebook profile, or writing a blog, ask yourself what your social strategy is: Who will see this information? How will this information be interpreted? What does this information say about you? How can this information help or hurt you? In the book *Rework*, Jason Fried and David Heinemeier Hansson said, "Marketing is not a department." Answering a phone, sending an e-mail, responding to a complaint, clearing a counter—it's all marketing. [Marketing] is the sum total of everything you do."[6] The same goes for the digital space—every post, every comment, every photo—it's marketing *You*.

Social networking is not going to go away. Facebook is topping 500 million users; LinkedIn is hitting 80 million; Twitter has 180 million users—the numbers are a testament that social media has woven its way into our daily lives. Qualman cites in *Socialnomics,* "In less than three years, social media became the most popular activity on the Web, supplanting pornography for the first time in Internet history. Even search engines weren't powerful enough to do that."[7]

The Web keeps us informed and keeps us connected, but when we engage online, we tend to forget we are operating in a public forum. Recruiters and employers love it too. They are searching Google, Bing, and other social network sites to see what articles you wrote, reading your blog, taking a look at awards or accolades associated with your name, evaluating the groups and/or communities with which you are affiliated. MetLife's Ian Decker said, "Candidates, or people who are just using LinkedIn from a networking perspective, don't even realize that they are putting their information out there and making themselves available for recruiters to go target them. Candidates are saying, 'Oh, this is great, a lot of information, you know I want to be connected to all these people.' And what they don't realize is that recruiters are saying, 'Go ahead, put more information out there, so I can see who you are.'"[8]

So you need to take control of the message. We suggested earlier that you should ask for help when first venturing into a digital space, but we also think that many of the social networking sites are intuitive— self-explanatory, in fact—so it's not difficult to figure out how to set your privacy settings. Don't tell yourself, "I'll do that later." A recent Microsoft Study found 70 percent of surveyed HR professionals in the United States (41percent in the UK) have rejected a candidate based on an online reputation.[9]

Even if you are not digitally engaged

The more advanced you are in your career, the more vigilant you need to be. "I think that people who are well respected in their fields and have made a contribution in their field should really take the time to formally approach this and utilize their networks in the way they do it traditionally. They would be far better off,"[10] said

Laurie Byrne, vice president, Global Staffing and Talent Development at Stryker Corporation. If you have a reputation in your field, your digital brand should augment your offline brand. The problem is that many older folks, if they are not actively engaged in the digital space, don't even realize they may have an online brand. Kellogg's Carolyn Rice said, "When I was first interviewing with the VP of HR here, I mentioned that we grew up in the same area. He looked a little surprised when I said this. Then I mentioned later during the interview that he was speaking at a certain conference in the upcoming month and he looked shocked. I said to myself, 'Oh shoot, I shouldn't have said this during the interview,' but I learned later that after the interview the VP went out to the people in his department and said, 'Do you know that she Googled me?' He did not know that he had an online presence, even though he had written all these white papers and spoke at a lot of conferences."[11]

Maybe you have currently downshifted and you don't think this applies to you. If you dropped out of the workforce to raise a few kids or retired early to begin a second career as a baseball umpire or you quit your corporate job to grow organic eggplants on that patch of land down south, you might feel totally justified in letting off a little steam digitally. You might want to burst out of all those constraints and have a little fun. It might be tempting, but we don't recommend it. Anything could change—and probably will—and you might have to reinvent your work self yet again, especially if you're healthy and you plan to live to age 100. Scott Taylor, owner and general manager of a McDonald's chain, said, "We won't go online and look up information on every hire, but for my key hires and people in manager positions, we need to do our due diligence to make sure that we are hiring the right employees."[12]

You can still have some fun

Step 1: What do you want your online brand to say about you?

The product is you. To have a truly effective digital brand you need to be authentic, but you also need to recognize that the minutiae you share can add up to a full-bodied portrayal of the unconscious you—whether it is through photos that provide an inside glimpse, via microblogging of what's happening every hour, through blogs that focus on your passion; through groups you associate with on Facebook or LinkedIn, through applications you download through companies where you have worked, through friends in your network—these are all things that create your digital brand. Make sure you are fully aware of what you are doing.

Many social networks urge you to create a motto. In Facebook, under your photo, it asks you to "write something about yourself"—an overview of who you are, a quotation that echoes what you are all about—again, another opportunity to develop your brand. You do not have to project some sterile android image to maintain your integrity online—no one will engage with you if you do—so have some fun. Give your brand some personality. Maybe you are an engineer but you love French cooking or Italian films, or you play ukulele in a bluegrass band. If you are creative, show your flair—show us a photo of your latest sculpture. If you are analytical, your online resume might showcase some intricate projects that display your accomplishments and strengths. The strongest personal brand is one that is consistent both online and offline; one carries over to the other.

You are human, but do yourself a favor, if you wake up on the wrong side of the bed, go back to sleep—do not go to the computer. "I am a big believer in personal brand, but those things can be really, really hard to shake if you get a negative one,"[13] said Mike Rickheim of Newell Rubbermaid.

Step 2: Think about your audience

You've established your digital brand and next you need to think about your audience: When you write, are you thinking of your friends, family, or work associates? They have to read this stuff. Will they appreciate it? Recently, on Twitter, a friend said, "My baby has cancer." We knew she was talking about her rabbit, but we're pretty sure the rest of the world didn't. And where are you going to post information? It might be time to ask: to blend or not to blend? That is the real question going forward. From the experts we spoke to, this matter is controversial. Host's Lisa Whittington said, "You're asking for trouble"[14] if you blend, but SAIC's David McMichael predicted that "You'll see a merging of the two. You'll see each side of the line inching that much closer."[15] So it will be a personal decision on how comfortable you are blending your work self and your personal self, but you do have options.

If you lead a Jekyll and Hyde existence, maybe it's important to keep your personal and professional lives separate. Consider creating two different digital profiles by using different screen names, often done by public personalities or those who are in professions in which it is important to have a very clear and separate line. For instance, a school teacher may want to engage with her students, their parents, and the community on a social network, but she might not feel comfortable having her college girlfriends posting stories about the good old days at the same site. It would be a good idea for her to create two separate Facebook profiles—using, for example, a married name for one and a maiden name for the other. "I think it is more appropriate to keep it separate. While balancing the two profiles may be somewhat administrative, it allows you to also balance and control the information and content that you share in your professional life,"[16] said Martin Cepeda, senior university recruiter at a Fortune 500 healthcare company. And don't forget that some companies have policies about what you can and cannot say about them online. Don't ignore these policies. Your free speech will likely get trumped—and you'll be out of a job.

Another option is to use different sites for different audiences. Having two different profiles can be a lot of upkeep, and, as they say, less is more. But we are getting more and more adept at juggling all our digital protocols. Remember when passwords used to throw us into a tizzy because we couldn't remember the 50 we had created? It took some time, but we pared down, and we can almost recite those 10 passwords in our sleep now. If you do decide to separate the professional from the personal, it may be confusing at first, but you'll soon get comfortable; at the very least you'll feel as though you have a little more control. Ian Decker added: "I'm on Facebook, so I know that there's all these privacy settings. If you are not good at that, and you don't want people to see your information, and you don't know how to brand yourself appropriately, you could be hurting your brand by not representing yourself well. I try to keep LinkedIn for my professional networking and Facebook strictly personal."[17] The last approach is to keep it blended. This may be a generational issue. Many of our experts said baby boomers and Gen Xers are a little more reluctant about blending the two. In other words, the older we are, the more private we tend to be. It may be that with longer histories we have more to keep out of public view. Or maybe we just understand the consequences better. Whatever the case may be, the younger generation will probably set the standard—they are, after all, the ones who brought us to social networks in the first place, and pioneers usually end up calling the shots in the long run. But, right now, you should know that not everyone likes the warts-and-all exposure. UPS's Matt Lavery said, "I have a dichotomy about that. I see the Facebook and Twitter. I see all these things, but I don't like it. I don't want to put myself out there that way. I don't have a Facebook page. I guess I'm more private. And I have a Twitter account—and I follow people—but I don't have a lot of tweets. Maybe it's a generational thing. Maybe it's a personal thing. Some people are very comfortable putting their entire life out there. Some people are not."[18]

Step 3: Where will you have an online presence?

After you decide whether you will blend or not, you need to determine which sites are the best for your brand. If you are starting from scratch and don't have a social networking presence, you may be asking yourself, where do I start? There are a ton of social networking sites, and choosing a few can be overwhelming. You don't want this to turn into a full-time job. During our interview process with Fortune 500 professionals, the sites with the most bang for the professional buck turned out to be LinkedIn, Facebook, and Twitter. Newell Rubbermaid's Mike Rickheim said, "I think LinkedIn is the best way to start. It has the most clearly defined strategy around linking up professionals. I think a lot of companies, including ours, are still trying to figure out how to best use a Twitter or Facebook or

MySpace as a recruiting tool. But LinkedIn is a great way to stick your toe in the water."[19]

If you are not a beginner and you are taking a bigger initiative with creating a digital social self and brand, you might decide to create a Website or a blog or post videos on YouTube. You can be as ambitious as you want. But whether you have an online presence or are just starting to create one, take the time to think about what you want your online brand to say about you, who your online audience is, and where you want your information displayed. Search your name across Google and Bing, and the sites where you have a social presence when you are not logged in, to make sure all the information out there is accurate and casts you in a positive light. Update frequently to make sure the good news far outweighs the bad. And, if you do stumble and things do cascade out of control, remember to take responsibility for it. As the authors of *Rework* reminded us, "Don't think you can just sweep it under the rug. You can't hide anymore. These days, someone else will call you on it if you don't do it yourself. They'll post about it online and everyone will know. There are no more secrets."[20]

Chapter 6

Networking With Your Virtual Cohorts

I think your network is very important, perhaps the most important thing you have when you're finding a job.
—*David McMichael*
Assistant Vice President and Manager
Staffing Strategies and Programs
SAIC

You've been networking forever, starting when you were just a kid. Remember all your can't-live-without buddies from school and summer camp? Every waking moment you were with them or at least thinking about them. You couldn't buy an album or a pair of shorts without consulting them. You were on the same wavelength and they meant everything to you.

And then something happened. You graduated, you moved, you changed. You lost touch.

Keeping track of your connections through time took effort—the phone calls, the letters, the random visits. Unless friends were a part of your daily life, most drifted away. Sometimes that was a good thing; often it was not. But it was inevitable. When you no longer share the day-to-day experiences, your acquaintances can lose some relevancy.

Once e-mail came around, it became a little easier to keep in touch with people. You didn't have to run to the drugstore for a card or the post office for a stamp or argue about the charges for long-distance telephone calls. You actually could keep relationships alive by dropping a short e-mail here and there to check in on all those friends and acquaintances from your glory days. It was convenient, simple, and friendly—even if you didn't like all the spam. Then, from the mouths of college-age babes, along comes social networking—a tool custom-made for keeping track of large and often disjointed networks. All of a sudden, your best friend from third grade gets to see a video of you doing your first parachute jump, or your old pal from Human Resources asks you to meet her for coffee the next time you visit your mother in Chicago. As Mike Troiano told us, "Social networking is just networking on steroids."[1]

Social networking then organically shifted to the job market. It was a natural fit. Networking has always been a critical component of finding a new job. Statistics vary, but approximately 75 percent of available jobs are filled through personal connections—and we're not referring to the owner of the company who plants his first-born in the finance department. Rather, networking is the friend of a friend who alerts you to an opening—and then speaks up on your behalf to help you come on board at a new company.

Unisys's Abigail Whiffen told us about a recent experience she had with networking. She said, "Candidates have different levels of savviness when it comes to leveraging social media. It varies by candidate and the role they're looking at. I can think of a candidate right now, who saw a job posting that I had asked for an MBA grad and he looked at the name on the posting, went into LinkedIn, looked at my profile and saw that we had a connection in common. Rather than reach out to me directly, he reached out to my law school classmate, who contacted me, and I said, 'Apply for the job.' It certainly helped me to look at his resume faster."[2]

Prior to social networking, managing a large network to leverage a position was challenging. Historically, we have been limited in the number of people we can skillfully maintain in our network. Meeting for coffee, attending a bridal shower, visiting your aunt's former boss, showing up at a basketball game, and arranging dates for informational interviews takes time. During our conversation with Shally Steckerl, executive vice president at Arbita, he spoke about the Dunbar number of 150. "Robert Dunbar was one of the first people to publish studies about the concept of how many human beings you can have in a tribe. It was an anthropological study. His research validated that the most successful and healthiest of tribes grew only to the size of 150 people. We as humans have evolved to be able to support relationships, significant relationships, outside of that number." Social Networking sites are the tools that allow us to now manage our network and easily reconnect with people we grew up with, went to school with, or worked with. "We've gone from unable to connect with, or have relationships with more than 150 people, to a multiplier effect of that based on how efficient we are able to utilize tools," continued Steckerl.[3]

As part of our research, we re-examined our own histories to see how networking had played into our careers. Brenda worked as a journalist, writer, and editor, and Coleen has worked most of her career in Internet sales. Both of these fields require strong networks, which are critical to success. The relationships that developed over time contributed enormously—both personally and professionally—to our lives and our livelihoods. For instance, Brenda's electronic network was instrumental in her last project. Working with Mary Ederle Ward, she also teamed up with AP sportswriter Tim Dahlberg, having never met him face-to-face, to write a biography about Gertrude Ederle, called *America's Girl*. In fact, she did not know what Tim looked like until she started to "follow" him on Twitter halfway through the writing project. To this day, although she considers Tim a valued member of her network, their relationship is entirely electronic. She has never shared a cup of coffee with him, yet she was able to coauthor a biography with him by collaborating digitally.

Coleen's network has been equally pivotal in her career. For instance, with the exception of her first job out of college, every one of Coleen's jobs thereafter was facilitated by her vast network. Not once did she have to rely on a third-party recruiter. Coleen recalls how she utilized her network to find the next opportunity:

My first "real job" job after college was working for a company called Lois Paul & Partners. I worked on the East Coast for three years and focused on high-tech public relations, and then I was relocated to San Francisco. Netscape and Marc Andreessen were getting a lot of press at the time. I was intrigued. One morning, I went to a Business Wire Breakfast because I wanted to find out more about what was going on and I thought these breakfasts were good opportunities to network and gather information. The topic that morning was CNET: The Computer Network, and Stacy O'Connell was the speaker. At the time, CNET was touting itself as the "MTV for the Computer Generation." It sounded like a fun place to work. When I got back to the office, I started to talk to different people in my network to see if anyone knew someone at CNET. I knew there had to be a connection somewhere. While talking to Ken Rutkowski, who had a radio show, "Tech Talk," I asked him if he knew anyone at CNET. He connected me with Patrick Toland at CNET. Next thing you know, I was working for CNET.

While at CNET, I met a lot of dynamic people. After working there for nearly three years, I was at a party with coworkers when Jill Robinson told me she was jumping ship at CNET and joining Excite. She told me I would be a great fit for the new group that Excite was creating and asked if I would be interested in interviewing. That week, she arranged an interview at Excite. I spent the entire afternoon and evening interviewing. That's how I met Evan Rudowski, who was getting ready to move to London to head up Excite Europe. During the interview, I joked that once I got this job, I would be calling him down the road for a job in Europe. A year and a half later, I was working for Evan in London.

Excite was one of the first Internet giants to close its doors when the Internet bubble burst. I worked through several rounds of layoffs but knew it was just a matter of time before the ax would fall on me. I stepped up my networking and while I was talking to an old client from CNET, E.J. Vongher, I mentioned that once I was laid off that I wanted to take a year off from the digital universe to pursue a field I loved—

the movies. Living in San Francisco, there aren't a lot of movie industry options, so I focused on Mill Valley Film Festival
and LucasFilm. I asked E.J. if he knew anything about these
organizations. The next day, E.J. emailed me a listing from
Craigslist that Mill Valley Film Festival was hiring. Because
they were advertising the job on Craigslist, I immediately sent
my resume and then sent an e-mail to people in my network
who might know someone at Mill Valley Film Festival. A
friend gave me the name of the hiring manager (LinkedIn was
too new to be on my radar screen). That's when I called Joni
Cooper at Mill Valley Film Festival and asked if she had filled
the position. She said she was still interviewing. I took a deep
breath and asked for a time that we could meet.

I got the offer the same day I got my pink slip from Excite@
Home—perfect timing! Mill Valley was a short-term contract
job, so I needed to focus on the next project, LucasFilm. An old
friend and coworker, Ken Phipps, freelanced for LucasFilm and
his wife, Karen Rose, also worked there, so I called them. Karen
was ready to go on maternity leave for six months, prior to the
launch of *Star Wars: Episode II*, and she needed someone to
cover for her. I met with her supervisor, was hired temporarily,
and worked on the PR team for the launch of the film.

I got a bird's eye view of the film industry, and had a great
experience, but I knew my future was tied to the Internet, so
I sent an e-mail to friends and colleagues yet again. An old client and current friend, Carrie Tice, responded immediately.
I had a job within a week. I worked for IGN for several years
and then decided to work for a larger company—Yahoo!.
My friend, Lucinda MacDonell, worked there, so I called her
to inquire about opportunities (while I was at CNET I had
helped Lucinda find a position) and she put me in touch with
Patricia Neuray and Marc Cote, who had an opening on his
team. I landed the job.

While at Yahoo!, I got engaged, and as a result had to relocate to Los Angeles. I reached out to an old coworker from
CNET and friend, Leigh Tolson Reichly, who recommended me
to Carol Terakawa, the regional vice president of the Yahoo!
Santa Monica office. I flew out to California and met with

Carol and her boss, Dave Dickman. Prior to the interview, I found out that Dave worked with one of my old coworkers, Ronnie Planalp, and thus I had Ronnie reach out to Dave to put in a good word for me. My network again proved invaluable as I was able to secure the Sales Director job at Yahoo! and join my fiancé in L.A.

Coleen's networking history is not as intricate and involved as it may seem at first glance. Basically it followed a typical pattern: She got her CNET job through a personal telephone call; her Excite job was the result of attending a social event; she relied on an old client-turned-friend (blurring the lines of personal and business) for her next position; she found the Mill Valley Film Fest job on Craigslist and reached out to her network for information about the hiring manager; she then tapped into the whereabouts of a former coworker for her job at LucasFilm; sent a mass e-mail to her network for IGN; and finally asked an old friend to return the favor and introduce her to a hiring manager at Yahoo!

Coleen's networking was crucial to her career, but it's essential to keep in mind that her networking was ongoing; it didn't start when she needed a job and it didn't end when she found a new position. She consistently built relationships—giving and taking equally—but always remaining alert and responsive to new opportunities and new people. It became part of her work ethic. Shelley Bird, executive vice president of Public Affairs for Cardinal Health, reiterated the idea that networking should be a critical aspect of a job, when she said, "You have to build those connections across the organization. I think people work at it here. It's a lot easier to collaborate when you've looked someone in the eye...you have a chance to meet them in person and get to know them, so we see a lot of value in that. In terms of the culture here, I think that's encouraged."[4]

Walk and talk, build friendships and associations, get to know the people you spend eight hours a day with, even if your cubicle or office is oh-so-comfortable. And, of course, you need to step up your efforts when considering a career move. Each of the Fortune 500 participants emphasized the importance of a network and how having someone internally at a company as your sponsor is a huge differentiator. "One thing is, as most people in Corporate America know, and it may seem disheartening a little bit, but often people's jobs and careers are built on who they know, not what they know. I am not saying that people aren't talented, but it is often because of their network that they get the best opportunities,"[5] said Chris Nutile, director, MediaLink Executive Search.

Building communities is not new. We are social creatures and we have developed networks since the early days, but, traditionally, we relied on family, friends, and business associates in the immediate community or day-to-day "tribe." What social networking allows us to do is enhance the network to include all those friends of friends of friends—anyone who can vouch for you, even in a remote way, and in warp speed. "Social Networking allows you to connect with someone much more quickly. Sure, you can exchange an e-mail with somebody, and you could do that 10 years ago, but now you can find someone on Twitter, on Facebook, on LinkedIn, and on any number of sites, which allows you to keep ties with them a lot more easily,"[6] SAIC's David McMichael said.

Who doesn't want to help others? It's good karma, after all, but there are still those who get a little queasy when it comes to networking. Networking may seem self-serving. It may seem artificial. It may seem opportunistic. All of those things can be true, if you just *use* your network and never reciprocate. "I would say that there is nothing more distasteful and frustrating than when you don't hear from someone for three to four years and you get an e-mail and they are looking for a job. That is what you are talking about abusing your network,"[7] warns Chris Nutile. We don't recommend that. But, even if a networking experience left a bad taste, we still think you need to give it another chance. Used correctly, a network can be highly productive.

It's a competitive job market; companies are doing more with less, so even if your attitude toward networking is negative, you need to revisit this. We understand that it can be a stretch for you to ask for help. We suggest you stretch anyway. And if it's a stretch for you to acknowledge others who have helped you in the past, please stretch again. Stretching can make all the difference. "I think those who care for individuals are people who have had the same experience, so even if you are out of networking shape, join alumni groups in your current company, your previous company, a sorority, or school. There are so many groups out there. You do have a common bond. I believe that bond is one of the most effective networking tools that you will ever find,"[8] said Laurie Byrne, vice president of Global Staffing and Talent Development at Stryker Corporation.

Another feature of social networking for the networking faint-of-heart is that this type of networking may soften the dread you may have about face-to-face or the telephone, where you may have to guard your reaction when you hear news that you don't like. Social networking provides a comfortable distance—for both parties—so get connected. You don't want to come across as someone who is out of the loop. Unum's Karen Bradbury mentioned a recent incident: "Just recently I spoke with someone who had asked for an informational interview and he was looking to do some networking. Before we actually spoke, I wanted to get more information on his background. He wasn't on LinkedIn at all, which surprised me. He's out there networking and he's out there trying to find a job, and it surprised me that he wasn't on LinkedIn, as I think it can be very effective in the networking process."[9]

And if you refuse to set up an account on LinkedIn on the grounds that your mother may try to link with you, then by all means choose another platform. Arbita's Shally Steckerl told us, "LinkedIn is not new. I mean the concept is not new. It started in 2003. In 1997–98, there were already online networking sites. In 1998, there was a company called 6 Degrees." So while the concept isn't new, Shally went on to tell us, "With the adoption of social media, more and more people are using things like…Facebook more…than anything else; there's 500 million people on Facebook. It's becoming easier to reconnect with people and keep your network alive."[10]

Some of you may be reluctant to use social media because it is rapidly evolving and there's a chance that the minute you figure out how to use one site, another one will usurp it. Starting all over again seems more trouble than it's worth. That's a valid fear, but it is probably more indicative of the disruptive world we live in. Everything is changing rapidly. We need to stay flexible. We also need to be committed to lifelong learning. We asked UPS's Matt Lavery what his company's preference was as far as social media goes. He said, "I don't know if I'm smart enough to tell you. You don't know in this kind of medium what's going to drop or take off. You don't want to get left behind. That's why we're carefully being a part of all of them. We made a conscious decision not to go to MySpace because it's really hard to control the content on that. I don't know what Twitter is going to be a year from now, but I think Facebook and LinkedIn are somewhat similar. I don't think we would ever want to pick one."[11] So, if it's any consolation, even employers aren't sure where social media will go from here, but most of them already know the dangers of not staying fully engaged with the next technological shift. "We are now creating a division between the ones who can communicate and the ones who cannot. The new threat is the digital divide—where devices talk to each other. Four billion people use mobile devices to connect,"[12] Arbita's Shally Steckerl said. There will always be more to learn, but even if you go into social media "kicking and screaming," as Laura Terenzi Khaleel from Pitney Bowes did two years ago, "[You] must begin, and I would begin slow and small and targeted."[13]

Fareed Zakaria, in "How to Restore the American Dream," writes about how "[Americans] fear that we are in the midst of not a cyclical downturn but a structural shift," and in the same article, he quotes Louis Gerstner, the former CEO of American Express and IBM, who said, "Most jobs that will have good prospects in the future will be complicated. They will involve being able to juggle data, symbols, computer programs in some way or the other, no matter what the task. To do this, workers will need to be educated and often retrained."[14] Now, more than ever, technological know-how is essential, and it would be a good idea to stop resisting it. That goes for social networking, too. Don't dismiss it before you even understand it.

If you are ready to boost your networking capacity via social networks, here's a suggestion from Mike Troiano: "First, invest some time in your profile. Upload a picture, for God's sake. Add a bio. Create some content to give people a sense of who you are, what you can contribute, what you'll be looking for. Then start to reach out to the people you know. Connect with them and start the dialog. Then reach out to people you don't know, but find interesting in the context of that network. Different social networking platforms have different rules and mores, but I think those are the common threads."[15]

Some additional tips include making sure that all of your information is complete, such as education, previous employers, and offline and/or online groups, as these will allow you to go through the names of other people within those groups so that you can review and possibly make a connection with an old friend or associate. Laurie Byrne, vice president of Global Staffing and Talent Development at Stryker Corporation, recommends, "Most companies, especially in the Fortune 1,000, have an alumni site for most of the people who have worked there. If you look at companies—even accounting firms—they even post their alumni sites right on their company sites because it utilizes their alumni to recruit."[16]

At the end of the day, that's what networking is all about: connecting with people who have shared experiences and passions. Engage. Read blogs. Stay current and connect. Give and take. This can be done online and offline, but social sites can help you use your network in a more useful and meaningful way by broadening your reach. Troiano adds, "Business is about relationships. And today there is simply no better or more efficient way to seed, cultivate, and harvest those relationships than social networking."[17] And, just in case you need a few more suggestions, implement the following steps into your strategy:

1. **Do not become so single-focused on the task at hand**—your very important work—that you neglect your network. It is an ongoing process. Use every opportunity to have a conversation about what's happening in your field. If you meet someone, ask if you can link to them. Share industry news. Give out your business cards to everyone, including newcomers.

2. **Do not rush to make things happen.** UPS's Matt Lavery said social networking has to happen "organically" for it to be successful. Be prepared to participate in the give and take over the long run.

3. **Continue to build your reputation at work and treat people fairly.** Come across as a person worthy of trust, which

means refraining from gossip, back-biting, and whining, and instead collaborate, be a team player and share the glory. Let your reputation precede you.

4. **Follow up on everything and be responsive when people reach out to you.** If someone asks you for a reference or recommendation, do so promptly and only in good conscience. If, for some reason, you cannot recommend this person, then explain to the person that you are currently tied up at the moment. Do not let them linger with a maybe.

5. **Share informative or even amusing links with others.** Get on their radar screens so that they know you are around. Watch carefully how other admired coworkers do it. Ask them if they had any strategies that were particularly good.

6. Often people make blanket requests via social networking: "Could you put a good word out there for me?" Anyone? This kind of approach is not very effective. Much better to **connect individually and ask**, even if the threat of rejection is a little higher. Again, this goes back to being specific and clear.

7. But the other side of the coin is to be helpful—even in those instances where fear prevents the other person from asking you specifically to do something. If you are asked to vote for your colleague's son's new band in an online competition, take the two minutes to **stretch yourself as an act of goodwill.**

8. **Attend industry functions. Mingle.** Be interested in others. When online, follow discussion threads; engage with others in online communities and forums, even if their opinions differ from yours. Welcome diversity. Steve Shapiro, the author of *Personality Poker,* said, "Opposites often repel, but this often produces innovation."[18]

9. **Volunteer for projects that are out of your comfort zone—** both in work and out of work. Work on a project that builds bridges in the organization or provides solutions to sticky situations or makes other people's jobs easier or more efficient. Help coach a team, build a community garden, organize a trip for seniors or disadvantaged school children.

10. **Take every networking opportunity your company offers
    and challenge yourself to make inroads within the organi-
    zation.** Collaborate with people outside your department.
    Get to know people in your organization who are work-
    ing on projects that interest you—and ask if you can help
    in any way. Attend functions—happily—whether they are
    going-away send-offs or birthday celebrations. Be human—
    even when you are at work.

11. But, *before* connecting, keep in mind Ken Nussbaum's rec-
    ommendation: **"Make an effort to keep your online pres-
    ence current.** If it is outdated, fix it. On occasion, I've come
    across online information (whether a Website, blog, LinkedIn,
    Facebook, etc.) only to see that the information is either very
    outdated or simply incomplete—or the most recent posting
    is from six months ago. It makes me wonder what happened
    to that person. I'd also recommend that the individual in-
    clude information that will not become stale shortly after
    it is updated. Periodically Google yourself, just to see what
    others are seeing when they search for you. If you notice
    outdated information, make an adjustment."[19]

12. **Categorize your network and create a subgroup of people**
    who can function as your advisers. This is the group you
    use for career questions, recommendations, and advice.
    MediaLink's Chris Nutile described it this way: "At a closer
    level, your colleagues, your mentors and people you have
    worked closely with in your career. I think you need to take
    a much more personal or traditional approach here. It's
    all about communicating what you are doing, asking ques-
    tions, being there for them when they have questions, call-
    ing people up and going out to grab a coffee, to grab lunch,
    and sitting down with them with no intent other than to
    connect. To me, this is your professional support network,
    versus your social network. This is the smaller group—say
    20 to 25 people tops—who you commit and invest time to
    stay in regular contact with. You should genuinely respect
    and care about what's going on with them personally and

professionally. Set up alerts on Google or Yahoo! to find out when they are mentioned in the press, add a new entry to their blog, or even comment on the movie they saw last night. With that information, you can send them a note saying, 'Hey I saw this, this is great, congratulations. If there is anything I can do to help, let me know.' One online product out there I found is called Gist.com. Basically you can feed in your contact list and link it to Facebook or LinkedIn. What it does is act like a CRM as it looks at how often you e-mail people and it will tell you that you e-mailed people x many times in the past 30 days, but it also goes out and gathers information on the Web about those people, so that if there is a blog entry, mentions in the press, even a Facebook or Twitter update, you will have that info on your dashboard. Use this free tool to keep up to date on the members of your support network I was talking about. I think it is about looking at that group as people who support you and you support them. Using technology to be more efficient is wonderful. Send them a note when they tweet on the birth of their latest grandchild, or add a Facebook entry on their daughter's wedding. The time for nurturing and building your network starts before looking for a new role."[20]

13. **Talk about your passions and demonstrate your expertise** so that people know they can go to you for valid information. And expand your horizons. If you restore old cars, share that information. If you spent the last year working for Habitat for Humanity, talk about your role. Be open to new people too. Recommend others to your friends and colleagues, especially if they are looking for advice or suggestions.

14. A.B.N.—**Always Be Networking**—when you are on a plane, at the supermarket, or waiting for a friend at a restaurant or bar. Initiate conversations, as you never know if that person next to you could hold the key to your next job.

If you are shy, then be interested instead of interesting—people love to talk about themselves. Encourage them.

Chapter 7

Hunting for a Face-to-Face

The best way to find the right job for yourself is to narrow your search and to display yourself as the best candidate for the role, so a shotgun approach is only helpful if you're look-ing for general employment at a lower entry-level type of role. The more senior levels require specific experience.
—*Kirk Imhof*
Group Director
Ryder System, Inc.

There's that word again: *specific.* Time and again the Fortune 500 hiring professionals emphasized the neces-sity of targeting your job hunt, so that the position you are seeking fits your skills as well as your temperament. You might think that the more jobs you go after, the better your chances, but the opposite is more often true. Employers are looking for a near-perfect fit. Hiring and training are ex-pensive propositions, and, although there's a big selection of applicants looking right now, employers would prefer to make hiring decisions based on the right person for the right job.

Nowadays hiring can be complicated.

When the job market went electronic (about eight years ago), applying to a vast array of positions became easier. "Technology is so quick, you can send out 100 resumes, but are any of them meaningful?"[1] Brett Goodman, a recruiter for EdisonLearning, asked. Technology made it possible for a lot of half-interested and/or unqualified applicants to apply for anything that struck their fancy—and that in turn meant hiring managers had to sort through all those scanned resumes to find the hidden gem—the right person for the right job.

Activision's Lissa Freed said, "I think if you go back 10 years to the paper-resume model, it might have taken a lot longer to actually sort through [resumes] because you didn't have any of the tools you have now with resume databases and sites to really be able to keyword search or link to who is the most qualified, so you would have to filter through. But because so many people can apply or put themselves out there, it is a much larger database now. Before, you were usually relying on the resumes that were sent through the mail, which indicated it was a pretty active, interested candidate who took the time to send a paper resume and cover letter."[2]

Back then, in the pre-electronic world, you invested a few dollars and had your resume printed on fine stationery. If you had a hundred copies made, you were careful—and more thoughtful—about who got hold of one of your resumes. You didn't want to run out and risk another print run, at a considerable cost to your pocketbook. Then you spent some time at the library researching your local prospects. Then technology changed the rules of the game. If you were considering a new position, you could use the spray-and-pray method. The electronic process made job seekers giddy with all its cost-free options and opportunities, and digital tools combined with the Internet allowed job seekers to broaden their horizon so they could go after positions normally out of their range.

Compound this tendency of applicants to throw as many arrows out into the job market as possible with the recent economic slump and you've got a lot more misses than hits. Paul Marchand, vice president of Global Talent Acquisition at PepsiCo, explains the situation this way: "This is a very different model than say five, 10 or 15 years ago. If you start to spend time in the [digital] space in general, what recruiting is all about is this classic image of the funnel. You have all of these people wanting to come to your company and they are finding you through job boards, campus recruitment and career fairs, friends and family, search partners and all of the different sources, and they are coming in through this big funnel and eventually the job of the staffing function or the recruiting function—if they are good at it—is to take the funnel and narrow it down to the right people at the right place at the right time."[3]

You might be saying to yourself, "I've been out of work for six months and I'm not feeling particularly sympathetic to the employer's dilemma of infinite choice." No one could fault you for feeling this way, but perhaps a better way to look at it is, with all this competition out there for a limited number of jobs, maybe it's time to shoot for the bull's eye. That means, as we mentioned in earlier chapters, you have:

- Reflected on what the best possible position for you will be.
- Researched companies and industries.
- Writing your 30-second elevator paragraph about who you are.
- Targeted five (or a few more…just in case) where you might fit in well.
- Crafted a clear, concise resume full of keywords and accomplishments.
- Created a brand that carves out your personal niche and highlights your best self.
- Reached out to your thriving network.
- Become entirely ready to launch your attack.

Making it through the narrow funnel

Employers want you to want them—specifically. That's one of the reasons they dedicate resources to touting their brand. They're saying to you: This is who we are and what we care about. For employers maybe it's all about their growth, innovation, profit, and sustainability; or maybe it's a combination of some other things you discovered while doing your research. But for the most part, companies are specifically saying: Here are the requirements; now tell us if you're still interested in working for us. Employers broadcast these requirements through company Websites, job postings, Career Pages, applicant tracking systems, and social media.

Fortune 500 employers—and other visible and dynamic companies— also attract applicants with their brands. What's ironic is they provide you with myriad information to whet your appetite and then they actually want you to opt out if the company or the specific job is not a good fit for you. Ron Gosdeck, vice president of Global Recruiting at Unisys, said: "I get, on any given day, any number of unsolicited resumes. Basically I hand them to my administrative assistant and say, 'Send a standard letter,' which is, 'Thanks for your interest in Unisys,' and I direct them to the career Website. If they are just broadcasting that they want a job, I can't help them because I don't know what job they're looking for. I can invite them to the career site. They can build a profile. They can apply for particular jobs. And then we present them with the Unisys Data Protection Policy, so they know what we're going to do with their data; then if they don't want us to do that, then they can choose not to apply."[4]

In other words, please don't waste our time—or yours—if you are not willing to fall in line with who we are and what we value. PepsiCo's Marchand explains: "And one of the things that has been a challenge for people, especially with the advent of applicant tracking systems and the advent of online job boards, like Monster, HotJobs, and CareerBuilder, as well as all the initial Web 1.0 Websites, is that it drew more people...into the funnel, and it just created more and harder work. What we are trying to do and what other companies are trying to do in a progressive and innovative way is to definitely have people come to our site and come to our company portal to see who we are, check us out, but then after seeing us or experiencing us, after hearing about us and understanding our company, our culture, and what we are about, to sit there and say, 'You know, I could click this button and immediately become an applicant or candidate or put my resume into their database,' or, after reading all of this, to say, 'Wow, great company, doing really neat things, but not for me. I am better off over there.'"[5]

Michael Peltyn, a vice president of Human Resources at MGM Resorts International, recently sourced 170,000 people for 10,000 positions at ARIA in Las Vegas. With a "one-stop-shop employment center," his recruitment team was able to get everyone on board within a year. Peltyn said his company was drawn to "candidates who emphasized, 'I am interested in ARIA. I know you are a 67-acre campus. I know you are green-certified. I know this, this, and this.' It speaks to us. It says that this person wants to be here. As opposed to, 'I applied to six places. I am sure that one of them will pan out. I don't know which one.' I've been with this organization for 20 years and can tell you, when identifying our hires we sought personality and commitment to providing exceptional customer service."[6]

Swirling around the "funnel" may sound demoralizing, but it doesn't have to be, because—especially with the advent of social media—you can attain almost limitless access to a specific company and its culture. Investigate. You can be in the driver's seat if you put enough effort into the process. Say to yourself, "I want to work at ABC Company because I like what they do. Now I'm going to figure out how to market myself to this company." Take charge. American Family Insurance's Lisa Beauclaire said, "I often tell people that LinkedIn is a good way to reach out to people on a one-to-one. I tell people to opt in to our LinkedIn group because there are a lot of employees and alumni in there and then they can contact people in a particular area."[7] You can view "Day in a Life" videos about a company on YouTube or read about it on its fan pages on Facebook. Even the Career Pages have veered away from Web 1.0 and become more interactive. McGraw-Hill's Brian Jensen said, "We have what we call our talent networks on our career site, which allows people to sign up if they are not quite ready to come here yet, but they want to stay in contact with McGraw-Hill and hear about things periodically. They can join our talent network and we'll send periodic e-mails about happenings at the company and send a job from time to time to keep them engaged on an ongoing basis. And when they're ready, they can look more seriously and apply."[8]

Age of custom-made

The traditional tools of the job search—the resume and cover letter—used to be the primary weapons in a job seeker's arsenal, especially if you didn't know anyone personally at a company. But, whereas resumes and cover letters still matter, in the Web 2.0 world, you now have other implements at your disposal—like your thriving network, your personal brand, and your access to layers and layers of information. In the funnel, all of these tools are prerequisites. And it takes time. With social media, you need to build, engage, and investigate.

Which means blasting a generic resume and cover letter out to 100 disparate employers just doesn't cut it anymore. Instead, it's so much more effective if you customize your strategy and rearrange your line of attack, which may mean tweaking your career objective on your resume each time you apply for an open position and writing a cover letter specific to the targeted company and position. EA's Cindy Nicola said to "use different resumes to apply to different roles,"[9] and Martin Cepeda, a senior university recruiter at a Fortune 500 healthcare company, emphasizing again the structural complexity of large corporations, suggested, "Most corporate career Websites allow for a candidate to attach multiple resumes and files to their profile. This allows a candidate to support his/her candidacy in greater detail by submitting supporting documents based on the job type and/or description. Submitting a more individualized and tailored application should help candidates get their applications noticed as it highlights their skills and experiences in specific relevance to the position(s) that they are applying for."[10]

This is one of the reasons why we waited until Chapter 7 to talk about cover letters. It's really important nowadays to do your research—via the Internet, trade journals, informational interviews, and social media—before you write a specific cover letter to a targeted company. You should have a ton of information by now that can attest to why you are an excellent fit for the open position. Your 30-second pitch paragraph can be used (you might have needed that earlier when you were actively networking), but it doesn't rank first in the cover letter. Your interest in the company does.

So typically this is how you need to arrange your cover letter: You should have a name of an individual. Remember, this is how social media can really help you drill down into an organization. Sean Splaine, a leadership recruiter for Google, suggested, "Do searches on Google to find people's e-mail addresses. For example, if you wanted to find my Google email address, you could do a simple search on Google like this: @google.com, e-mail. It will bring you a lot of hits, but you will soon find several e-mail addresses pop up, and first initial, last name@google.com would be the email code we use."[11] Take the extra hour to do this. It can make all the difference in the hunt.

The second item on your agenda as far as the cover letter goes is to write that killer paragraph about why you want to work at a particular company. Maybe the employer just won an award; maybe the company is expanding in a region near you; maybe the company has just acquired a new division. Whatever it is, show that you are interested in that particular business. Avnet's Claudia Reilly said, "If you see a long e-mail [cover letter] that's four paragraphs, you're more likely to not read that. You might read it eventually. But if you write three-sentence paragraph that says, 'I would love to work at Avnet. I'm impressed with your revenue growth,' something that grabs their attention to read more…you have to say the best thing possible in the top half to keep them reading."[12]

The authors of *Rework* think "Resumes are ridiculous," but they extol the power of the cover letter. "In the cover letter you get actual communication instead of a list of skills, verbs, and years of irrelevance. There's no way an applicant can churn out hundreds of personalized letters. That's why the cover letter is a much better test than the resume. You hear someone's actual voice and are able to recognize if it's in tune with you and your company."[13]

Actually, the Fortune 500 professionals we spoke to were split down the middle regarding cover letters. Many, especially at "younger" companies, said the cover letter would soon be a relic, but others at the Fortune 500 did not agree. Use your judgment—if you're applying to McGraw-Hill, skillful communication is probably highly valued; other companies may stress other competencies. What's essential to remember, though, is that everyone we spoke to emphasized that you need to be *clear* and *concise*. Avnet's Claudia Reilly said, "Say as little as quickly as possible."[14] Activision's Lissa Freed also echoed this sentiment when she dissed "too many words on a piece of paper.... They just don't read the detail."[15]

A few other Fortune 500 hiring managers had some other requirements for the cover letter. Debbie Mathew, a business strategic partner, Human Resources, at Hewlett-Packard, said, "One thing that not everybody does is identify how they got connected to the position. It is all about who you know. A lot of times, that is the reason that I will continue to look at the cover letter and the resume—if it was a friend of a friend. So I think that is important. I would like to know up front, why they are looking for the position. I like to know if the person is working or not working."[16]

So, once you have convinced the employer that you are interested primarily in working for that particular company, you can now cut and paste your 30-second pitch paragraph about who you are into the cover letter—as your second paragraph. Four or five lines, as we mentioned earlier, should do it. Remember, an employer wants you to be the solution to the company's problem.

Your cover letter will most likely be electronic, so read the following sample to get an idea of how it should be arranged and written.

Dear Ms. Smith:

I have admired your company's resiliency in an ever-changing marketplace and I just viewed "ABC Company's Customer Retention" on YouTube from your recent conference and exhibition in San Francisco. I was particularly impressed with your "Think global, act local" emphasis on direct marketing and your new ventures in India and Brazil. Your plan to merge direct marketing with transaction marketing is an area I am particularly interested in, and I would like the opportunity to meet with you to discuss ABC's marketing director position.

I have a strong background in the digital marketplace—on both the agency- and client-side. Having worked for a leading advertising agency as well as a Fortune 500 company, I have global experience and have been responsible for digital strategies, business development, marketing, and training. I am equally adept at customer communication management and creating cost savings. Currently I am managing the digital strategy of our site's largest account, developing innovative initiatives for the Web, social media, and mobile channels so that XYZ's clients can interactively communicate with their current and future customers.

Thanks for connecting with me on LinkedIn. If you would like to discuss my qualifications further, please contact me at (212) 555-5555. I look forward to hearing from you.

Sincerely,
Greg White

There's not an enormous amount of detail in the cover letter, but enough information to intrigue the hiring manager. How so? The applicant shows an interest in the company, encapsulates his work history, shows some gratitude for making the initial connection, and, finally, provides a telephone number to arrange a further discussion—or perhaps a telephone screen. In other words, the candidate has made the recruiter/hiring manager's life easy by being interested, knowledgeable, brief, polite, and a good fit.

Cover letters are about striking the right balance. A little about you, a little about me (let's talk further) is what you want to achieve. Weyerhaeuser's Stan Weeks said it's also about marketing: "You have got to know how to market yourself, and that can be a difficult thing just in and of itself. Someone could be very good at their job, but if they want to get inside a leading company, they have to know how to market themselves and share their experience and share what they've done. And that could be difficult for people to talk about how great they are and what a terrific job they've done."[17] We think Vincent Taguiped's suggestion may help. He said to avoid braggadocio and hype and instead be "confident" and "humble."[18] That balance can be a tricky mix for some people, but provided you are sincere, you should be able to pull it off.

Once the resume and cover letter are sent, prepare yourself for a telephone screen. It's that random telephone call you get just as you're stepping off the train. If you cannot talk without shouting, then politely ask if you can call the person back. In fact, you may want to do this in any event just to reset your focus—or refresh your memory. EdisonLearning's Brett Goodman said, "When I call someone for a telephone interview and that person says, 'What job is this?' well then that person has failed as far as I'm concerned. They just threw their resume and cover letter out there without even considering the specific jobs or company."[19]

Usually the generalist or manager in Human Resources is trying to ascertain your interest as well as your qualifications. Remember the pitch you wrote earlier? This is a good time to use it. Occasionally a telephone screen also brings up the topic of your salary range, especially if you didn't apply through an applicant tracking system. You may have an idea that you would like to make 10 percent more than you are making at your current job—that's reasonable—but you should also use the free salary wizard on *www.salary.com* to determine if that salary falls within the range of your profession in the area where the job is located. Just plug in your job title and zip code, and you'll get a good idea what you can expect. Whatever you do, don't pull a fantasy number off the top of your head and tell the manager that's what you want to make at your new job. That's not a professional approach. Throughout the job hunt, you need to know what you're talking about. At this stage of the process, hiring managers are looking for a range. Once the offer of a job is made you can use your negotiation skills to boost that number—provided it's reasonable.

Keep in mind that salary should not be the only consideration when weighing a job offer. There are many factors involved, such as cultural fit, affiliation, and whether you will be happy doing the work that is required. If the work is torture, you will have a hard time living up to your potential—even if the salary is exceedingly generous. Dan Pink, author of *Drive,* claims, as long as a company pays you fairly, then autonomy, mastery, and purpose—those intrinsic motivators—probably will carry much more weight in the long run.[20]

Chapter 8

Panning for Gold Employees

The thing with social media, it has to grow organically. You can't—unlike other types of advertising where you can spend more and more money to get your message out there to more and more people—in social media that's shunned in some respects. It has to grow organically or it doesn't grow.
—Matt Lavery
Manager, Corporate Workforce Planning
UPS

Recruiters are like gold prospectors who trek out into the vast wilderness with their heavy backpacks to search for the elusive treasure. So much depends on them finding gold, but it's always an iffy proposition. If they are lucky enough to find a rich deposit in a warm stream, they still have to pan through all the silt, sand, and gravel to unearth those sun-yellow nuggets. Even under the best conditions, they don't always strike it rich—although they are usually a little more fortunate than Humphrey Bogart was in *The Treasure of Sierra Madre*.

As a job seeker, part of your strategy should be to know how recruiters—these prospectors—find you. In many respects, you have to go to the same watering holes and mingle by participating on platforms that are favored by recruiters. It's also a good idea to know what tools they use to narrow the applicant pool. It will be a testament to your professionalism to know how the hiring process works, even at a particular company. This means you need to investigate continually and be proactive. As Vincent Taguiped, a manager of recruitment for a Fortune 500 media company, said, "Take ownership of your job search. So many people expect you to find a job for them. It is important to be aggressive and persistent, but it is not someone else's job to find you a job, as that responsibility ultimately lies with you."[1]

When you don't have a job or you're barely hanging on to the one you have, especially in a job market as competitive as this one, it's tempting to take the first job that comes along. A definite downside to this strategy is, if you dislike the job after six months, you're back at square one—unless you plan to bite the bullet and hold out for two or three years in an ill-suited job. Two or three years? That's the normal time span that indicates to a future employer that you're not a job-hopper. Six-month stints here and there are not going to enhance your career. And those years at a job you don't like will seem like a lifetime. Better to approach the job hunt with laser focus—and only accept the job offer if it's the right fit for you. Do your research and do not react to the pressure of impending unemployment. A job hunt is challenging but also manageable if you tackle this process rationally and take small, meaningful steps in the right direction.

The job hunt will require patience and it requires know-how. It also requires the following: having the right skills and experience, having someone who can help in your network (not required but certainly helps), having a well-organized resume that attracts recruiters so they want to know more about you, and having a good strategy—one that includes social networking. Provided you showcase your skills and qualifications in the best light, there's a good chance *recruiters will find you.*

That's a lot of Boolean logic

Provided you showcase your skills and qualifications in the right light, there's a good chance recruiters will find you. For instance, if your keywords tell an accurate story, they will find you through search. SAIC's David McMichael said, "We rely heavily on keyword searches—the Boolean logic[2] to drive the most targeted searches. Speaking on behalf of recruiters, and having been a recruiter myself, the stronger the search string, even on the social media sites, the better the results are going to be." At SAIC, recruiters are looking for "needle-in-the-haystack skill sets (there might be only 50 people in the world who have this special background),"[3] so very specific keywords are a must. But, according to Newell Rubbermaid's Mike Rickheim, generally it is better to use the kind of words that will expose you to "the broadest audience...the nomenclature that you use should be the kind that is recognizable to the layperson. For instance, if you go out and post your resume and only use terms specific to Newell Rubbermaid, chances are that those words are not going to be familiar to the other recruiters who are looking for you...so rather than calling yourself an MIS Lead III, which we see a lot of in the technology world, refer to yourself in a more common fashion—like IT Leader, Technology Leader, etc."[4] Based on these opposing viewpoints, you might be wondering what the best approach is in terms of keyword search—highly specific, or general all-purpose? Both McMichael and Rickheim have valid points. As in so many other aspects of the job hunt, it is up to you to decide—based on your targeted company and desired position—what tactic is best for you. When it comes to finding a new job, your research into what's required will make all the difference. If you are a highly skilled, needle-in-the-haystack professional, then the more specific keywords you use, the easier it will be for recruiters to find you. But if you are a marketing professional with innumerable transferable skills, you might want to broaden the search string—using keywords that allow you to move seamlessly from one job or industry to the next. You can make this decision safely *after* you have done your research and targeted your opportunities.

A favorite watering hole

If you create a professional profile, recruiters will discover you on LinkedIn. "The best advice I give to people looking for jobs is 'If you are looking for a job and you are not on LinkedIn, then you aren't really looking for a job.' When I first started on LinkedIn, I was a little unsure of how I was going to use it. I had a very basic profile. Then, I realized that it was a great way to do networking and marketing at no cost other than the time involved. Now, my feeling is that the more information I include, the easier it will be for people to find me. I've also joined a number of groups, including company alumni groups. After all, one never knows who might want to find you,"[5] said CPA Ken Nussbaum, of K. Nussbaum & Associates. Put as much effort into assembling a robust LinkedIn profile as you would in creating a resume. Pitney Bowes' Laura Terenzi Khaleel said, "If we're doing what we call direct sourcing, if we are networking on LinkedIn and we're working different groups we belong to on LinkedIn, we might be reaching out to candidates and having a phone conversation with them to really make them aware of the opportunity, get them interested, and have them agree to move forward."[6] Find out what groups your targeted company belongs to (research!) and engage in the conversation.

If you blend professional and personal networking—and you refrain from sharing your outlandish side—recruiters can find you on Facebook. "The demographic of Facebook is becoming a mature demographic. We see a rapid growth in the acceptance of Facebook as a platform for a professional and very experienced audience,"[7] said CSC's Jim Gattuso. With more than 500 million users, recruiters are monitoring Facebook very carefully. Facebook may eventually turn into one rich deposit of gold nuggets. "Facebook can become more and more useful because it has location-based search—LBS. Facebook has blogs, photo sharing," said Arbita's Shally Steckerl. He said he expects employers will eventually "host a career fair, advertise the career fair, post photos about the career fair."[8] And, according to EA's Cindy Nicola, another feature of Facebook for the job seeker is that it has "more than 700,000 local businesses with active Pages."[9] If you are interested in a smaller, local business, here's another opportunity to engage with a future employer.

Bird's-eye view

If you create a cohesive message, recruiters may reach out to you via Twitter. Unlike Facebook and LinkedIn, Twitter is a much looser network; in fact, it allows you to connect with hundreds or even thousands of "weak ties"—people you don't know personally—based on a shared interest. While Twitter is still evolving, it may turn out to be one of the more powerful platforms for the job seeker. Lisa Beauclaire, of American Family Insurance, said, "I think we're going to see a lot more of Twitter in the future because of all the mobile apps. Where mobile technology is now, I don't think many people are looking for jobs via mobile, but give it two years and, if mobile takes off, and I think it will, Twitter will be important."[10]

Individuals are using Twitter to build their brand. If you check out the most followed people on Twitter, Eminem and Lady Gaga take the lead. Yes, Lady Gaga is talking about dropping a false eyelash in her morning cup of coffee (Lady Gaga's tweet, November 21, 2010),[11] but they are also talking about upcoming concerts, products, recent awards, and accolades, demonstrating what a powerful PR and marketing tool tweeting has become. They know the importance of branding themselves. After reading *The Web 2.0 Job Finder,* you will, too.

With popularity soaring and tweeting turning mainstream, Twitter is an obvious place for recruiters to find prospective employees. (It's also an obvious place for you to find jobs. Just plug a location in the Search bar and see how many jobs in your area come up.) Recruiters are prospecting far and wide for you, especially if you have created an online persona that says you are a viable and appealing candidate. Twitter, with more than 190 million users, is growing daily—and quickly becoming a great vehicle to tap into the pulse of a company. Laura Terenzi Khaleel of Pitney Bowes said, "Twitter, for example, is big and it's out there and you have to utilize it as an employer for getting the word out about jobs.[12] Employers are using TweetMyJOBS, which is Twitter's largest job board, and it would be a good idea if you did too. Just set up a free account and narrow down jobs by industry, job type, and geography. Twitter also gives registered users a *Personal Branding Guide.*"[13] Get some exposure now—at no cost, other than time, to you. Khaleel added, "We utilize something called TweetMyJOBS, and that basically sends alerts to those who are looking for positions, who have opted in to receive these notices. Twitter definitely gets to a lot of those young folks who might be looking at non-exempt and entry-level positions."[14]

The Sunday classifieds

Companies are taking the money that they used to spend on newspaper ads and are now advertising, marketing, and promoting jobs online because people are "hanging out" online and it is proving to be a more economical—and focused—avenue to find talent. "I also think if you look at it from a budgetary perspective, social media has really changed how we distribute our talent advertising budget dollars. In fact, just this year alone, we saw a redirection for more than 30 percent of our total talent advertising dollars going toward social media advertising products,"[15] said David McMichael of SAIC.

As with all advertising and marketing, recruiters want to get the right message to the right people at the right time. An online environment provides recruiters with the ability to reach job seekers when they are looking for a job as well as the more passive users when they might not necessarily be looking but are open to hearing about interesting opportunities. "I think that the larger organizations that are starting to understand digital, and get how digital marketing assists recruiting, are already doing it. I am already seeing some of my colleagues take on roles focused on digital marketing for recruiting purposes. These are people who really understand the nuances of how to promote and market an employee brand without becoming annoying or doing it too often. They know how to segment different parts of their Twitter list or their different groups on LinkedIn, so instead of broadcasting and talking about engineering roles to salespeople, they talk about the sales roles to salespeople and the engineering roles to engineers and marketing to people in marketing,"[16] explains Chris Nutile, director, MediaLink Executive Search.

If you are saying to yourself, *This is all well and good, but the economy stinks and all those dream jobs are just fantasies,* have faith. As we already mentioned, employers did not stop hiring completely—they just hire differently when the pressure is on. They hire slowly and they also insist on a near-perfect match. As a job seeker, you need to figure out how you can transform yourself into that right match for your targeted company—this is not beyond your reach. You do not do this by inflating your qualifications or fudging your skills. Instead do this by rethinking and/or developing your assets; highlighting your transferable skills and zeroing in on the employer who needs you to solve its problem. Once you do, you will be surprised at how many recruiters start looking for you.

Not only that, but economic booms and busts tend to be cyclical— and it looks like the hiring freeze at a lot of companies is thawing. Claudia Reilly, national program manager at Avnet, said, "As social media was booming, hiring had slowed, so it will be interesting to see what happens in this next year, when both are booming. Now people will be using LinkedIn and the boards because there will be more openings. I think it was good timing because the social media networks needed to find their niche and do it correctly—and now that people have had a year to become familiar and comfortable with it—when all the jobs are going to start getting posted. I mean, even though there was stuff all along, it's going to double now. Business is getting better and hiring freezes are being lifted."[17]

As with every industry, competition to get the best employees is stiff and recruiters don't want to see good employees get away. That's why they are reaching out via social networks—where a large pool of technologically savvy applicants spends time. Chris Nutile explains that, "With regard to social media, there are two different things: (1) advertising and promoting from within a company, or (2) advertising and promoting an organization and branding it as what we would consider 'employer of choice' within a marketplace or within a specialty. As far as promoting opportunities and branding as 'employer of choice,' you know Facebook, LinkedIn are great for that. Having a social media team or specialist within the organization who maintains the social media strategy for the talent acquisition and recruiting teams is something that is very important now."[18]

While recruiters are using social sites and tools to find prospective employees, they will continue to use offline vehicles as well. In other words, traditional networking is still important; in fact, nothing is as good as a face-to-face conversation. With or without social media, you still have to hone your communication skills, you still have to go to career fairs and networking events, you still have to reach out to your network about your job hunt and tell them specifically what you are looking for. The beauty of social networking is it can help you move quickly, extend your reach, and build a complete package—You—that will enrich your value to a potential employer. But the point is to use every tool in your toolbox—whether it's 2.0 or not. Vincent Taguiped, manager for Recruitment at a F500 media company, reinforced this idea when he said, "Our company is using Facebook and tweets to attract and promote internship positions because it is a great avenue to reach a possible untapped audience. It has been a very successful program, so we are actually broadening it outside of internships. This won't ever replace traditional ways of advertising a job. It is a new added benefit, but it will not supersede the old ways."[19]

Social networking is not for everybody

To be effective in the social networking landscape, you need to be a good communicator as well as proficient at moving around in cyberspace. If you're a gifted engineer who prefers symbols to grammar there's a good chance you will avoid the medium. If you're an ace auto mechanic who thinks in nuts and bolts instead of A through Z there's a good chance you'll leave the computing to your wife or kids. If you're a traditionalist with an aversion to anything that requires a modem or even a plug you probably prefer your mailman to e-mail. If you are disadvantaged—without resources such as Facebook, Twitter, YouTube, MySpace, blogs, LinkedIn, Bing, Xing, hashtags, and Google, the Internet may seem like a foreign language. Social networking is not for everybody.

And that's an issue for both employees and employers. As companies wander into the social networking landscape, employers realize they still need to reach out to a diverse workforce, which includes people who have not embraced the medium. And, as social networking starts to become entrenched in the hiring process, some job seekers may risk being overlooked if they don't participate in the conversation.

The good news is that in a fairly short timeframe—a decade approximately—the American workforce has come to recognize that computer literacy is a prerequisite for almost all types of employment, no matter what the position (whether you are an auto mechanic or a research scientist). Everyone has more or less come on board as far as computers go. UPS's Matt Lavery told us about when the application process first got computerized: UPS decided to install more than 1,000 kiosks in employment offices throughout the country so it could reach out to a broad spectrum of employees. "What happened over the course of the first year or two is that we found they were not being used all that much because candidates were completing the application at home, coming in for the interview, self-scheduling, and going about the process the way we intended."[20] There's a good chance that the same will happen with social networking. Late arrivers can take advantage of the fact that the kinks have been ironed out; the boundaries have been established; the mistakes have already been made.

Social networking is still evolving, and many still consider it just the latest and greatest addition to an increasingly complex hiring process. Without a doubt, it will give you an edge when you're looking for a job right now, but you can still find employment without it—a LinkedIn profile is not yet a necessity. And you don't need an interactive resume to become a highly successful marketing manager. Everyone is still experimenting, so we have a ways to go before it becomes a hiring protocol. PepsiCo's Paul Marchand said, "A trend that was starting to get a lot of press was…'gone will be the resume, gone will be the paper document, the future will be video.' That hasn't happened, quite frankly. I don't think it will happen in the way those people, or that space, believe it will happen. One primary reason, I think individuals know that the message that they put out on video can hurt them. I mean, only some people are photogenic, only some people can get the words and the sentences and the expressions and the visuals all working at the same time."[21]

This is one of the reasons why companies rely on a whole array of steps to vet prospective employees—resumes, cover letters, personal recommendations, applicant tracking systems, telephone screens, references, face-to-face interviews, background checks. Many factors go into a hiring decision. PepsiCo's Marchand added, "On paper you can focus on the substance and not on how I am dressed, what I look like, what I'm wearing, what my physical appearance is, and then get me in the door based on my competency and credentials and my experience as opposed to the face and body that go with that. Bring me in, you still may have a bias toward me once you meet me based on my gender, based on my race, based on my physical appearance or based on the fact that I do well or don't do well in the job of communicating, but at least I have a shot at it."[22]

Employers know the value of having a diverse workforce. Newell Rubbermaid's Mike Rickheim said, "We are looking for the best people, regardless of where they come from."[23] Employers still need "solid worker bees," as Chris Nutile mentioned, and not necessarily all "rock stars"[24] or an "army of generals," as Cardinal Health's Shelley Bird said, to conduct their business successfully.[25] And most people have innumerable venues where they can fulfill their potential and feel validated—outside of their careers—and without doing it online. Social media is simply a tool to use when building a network; it certainly doesn't mean you can't make deep connections and form a viable network without it. Pitney Bowes' Khaleel said, "If I were out there looking for a position now (I come from a more traditional background and yet had to move into the more current social media because of my work), I would absolutely not ignore the good, old-fashioned, traditional networking strategies."[26]

Companies do reach out to a diverse workforce without tapping into Facebook and LinkedIn all the time. Ryder's Kirk Imhof said, "We're a large organization, and we hold ourselves to very high standards....We ensure our opportunities are made known and available to a very diverse population of candidates. This is accomplished via a robust outreach effort using Internet-based job boards, traditional media, social networking, and government job services. This is the predominant way we ensure our opportunities are visible to many." Imhof added, "We also have a number of ways we manage our applicant pool. For all positions, but especially for those positions that we are constantly hiring, such as drivers and mechanics, we encourage candidates to submit general interest into the company by creating a profile at ryder.jobs, informing us of their general skill set. Then we're constantly trying to help them get matched to our opportunities."[27]

Like minds produce like results, so diversity is an essential ingredient to fostering innovation, especially in a global marketplace, but as a workforce, we still have a ways to go before everyone is plugged in to social networking. Fortunately employers recognize this, and they continue to reach out traditionally as well. PPG's Shannon Pelissero said, "People need to feel that diversity is a true initiative. I know some people put it out there, but they don't inherently believe it. I think you need to be, first and foremost, genuine about your diversity initiative. It's not something you do just to talk the talk. You have to walk the walk."[28]

EEOC guidelines, which are worth reviewing as you job hunt, will continue to ensure diversity, but job seekers should think twice before they decide to opt out of social networking entirely. Remember what Louis Gerstner, the former CEO of American Express and IBM, said about the job market going forward. Employees will need to be able "to juggle data, symbols, computer programs in some way or the other, no matter what the task."[29] So that's all the more reason why you need to make an effort to improve your communication and tech skills (including social media) by making a commitment to lifelong learning. There's an excellent chance your future may depend on it.

When we asked Holland-Mark's Mike Troiano about whether social networking is necessary, he said, "Abso-freaking-lutely. But whether it's necessary or not, why would you not? It's just crazy to me. If someone's not involved in those media, I assume that person either has something to hide or they are a Luddite in their views regarding technology and communication. Neither is an attractive quality. I very rarely hire people who I don't know through someone. And it's better and faster for everyone if we can explore those mutual associations sooner rather than later."[30]

Chapter 9

If the Fit Works

In order to make a good, lasting match, where your perfor-
mance and engagement in the role are both very strong, you
need to match on both job skills and company culture—job
skills matching your experience and capabilities and culture
matching your affinities to a particular environment.
—Kirk Imhof
Group Director, Recruiting
Ryder System, Inc.

You are feeling pretty good because you have an interview next week. You are this close to landing a new
job; all you have to do is ace the face-to-face. This may be
an enviable position to be in, but you still have to jump
the biggest hurdle of the job hunt. If you have built up
steadily—taking your research vitamin daily—you have
a good shot at landing on your feet, but you should also
know that there are a few other obstacles that have to be
circumnavigated. For one, corporate fit. Shannon Pelissero,
an HR manager at PPG Industries, said, "I've seen many
candidates who have every qualification for the job and it's
just not a fit and they're not going to be successful. I think
at the end of the day, putting all the social media aside,
that's just what matters."[1]

Ryder's Kirk Imhof refers to this corporate "fit" as "affinity." Whatever you call it, it's a crucial piece of the hiring puzzle. Although we mentioned earlier that innovation often results from differences—rather than similarities—companies prefer to hire "like minds." Employers want you to feel comfortable in the corporate environment, so you can do your best work. If you are out of your element, there are just too many hurdles to jump. And let's face it, you want to be comfortable, too. If you're a laid-back, catch-you-later-man type character and the rest of your colleagues are I-need-it-yesterday personalities, you won't fit—and you'll be crawling in your skin counting the minutes until you can get out of the office every night at 5 p.m. sharp.

So how do you know if it's a fit? During an interview, it's the click that happens when you speak to people who are on the same wavelength—they understand you; you understand where they're coming from. At a minimum, most interviews usually entail meeting several people—the HR gatekeeper, the hiring manager, the big boss—so the click has to happen from top to bottom, but you get the idea. Even if you are feeling desperate to find a new job, and the company wants you on board because you have done a superb acting job, do not accept the offer if you have any doubts about working comfortably in that environment. It won't work in the long run—and you'll be doing another job hunt in six months to a year. Cardinal Health's Shelley Bird said, "It's probably more about the cultural fit than personality. Personality probably plays a part, but you are either comfortable in the culture in the organization or you're not. And I think people after a time probably decide whether it feels right for them. And that has a very direct impact on how they perform and the relationships they build. It's a reciprocal arrangement. It has to work for both the employee and the employer for it to be successful."[2]

A way to get around it?

The only way to get around corporate fit is to do your own research. In other words, you make the decision whether you can work well in that environment—instead of the other way around.

We know of one job seeker who did not go on an interview because she Facebooked (new verb like Googled?) the hiring manager and decided from the get-go that the fit was all wrong. It goes back to the idea of the funnel that we referred to earlier: all these people swirling around the funnel until the lucky few reach the opening. Essentially that's what recruiters are doing when they put you through the paces—seeing if you're a good match for the company. As you swirl, you should also be asking yourself those same questions. Up to this point, you have expended a considerable amount of effort gathering information, tweaking your resume, reaching out to your colleagues and friends; do not stop investigating just because you have a job interview next week. Keep fact-finding. It's fairly easy to do. Paul Marchand, PepsiCo's VP of Global Talent Acquisition, said, "You have to know the companies to which you are applying. You need to be informed. Those things are much easier than they were years ago. You used to have to mail away for an annual report or go to the library and get the one copy. All of that stuff is accessible online. The people who are using it are using it to their advantage. Other people are just saying, 'Okay, this is easy. Click. Send. Done.' The employer has a higher standard. We have all of this stuff on our corporate Website. We have a career site. We spend money. There are lots of media outlets for you to get Google alerts about us every day. You should know more than any candidates in the past. You should know more than our employees. Those who do, blow us away. And we are like, 'Wow, when can you start? You are already living the brand; you are already here.'"[3]

Sometimes we choose to ignore those alarm bells that go off after an initial meeting: the hiring manager who makes you wait 45 minutes to see him; the executive assistant who is rude; the employer who makes you jump through a hundred hoops to come onboard and then makes you jump through a thousand hoops just to get a simple $10 requisition signed later. Even though you are eager to start working, do not put your head in the sand. Remember what the authors of *Rework* said about marketing? Well, the same goes for the hiring process. Little things do matter. Take everything in when you walk through the doors for your face-to-face, which means you are listening furiously between sentences. You have to be quiet to hear the click, but it can make all the difference in job satisfaction.

Nine times out of 10, your best job interview will likely lead to your best job (and vice versa) simply because the fit was right to begin with.

Preparation is key

Many of you are probably convinced that a job interview is not an accurate picture of the new job. You still have to work with a variety of people (many of whom you will *not* meet during the interview); you still have to perform your specific duties (they can change from day to day even in a highly specific area); you still have to figure out your supervisor's managing style (maybe she was on her best behavior during the interview). No doubt about it, a lot can go wrong after you accept the offer. But, if you do as thorough a vetting of the employer as they do of you, your chances improve vastly for finding a job that is mutually beneficial.

Start by talking to insiders. CSC's Jim Gattuso said, "Just as we use LinkedIn to reach out to candidates, candidates can use LinkedIn to identify who works at different companies and to contact people at those companies and just have very open conversations."[4] Lisa Beauclaire, a specialist of Sourcing and Diversity at American Family Insurance, said she attends career fairs where she does employment marketing. It surprises her that the people she meets do not follow up with a telephone call. She said, "I'm handing out my card. Call me. That's my role. I network with people. And not many people call. People have been e-mailing a lot more though."[5] Think how effective it would be to call up the recruiter and just say, "Hi, I met you at the career fair and I was wondering if you could give me a little more information about the culture at your company. I'm planning to submit my resume via the applicant tracking system, but I just wanted to ask you a few questions first." That conversation makes an impression. Not only will you find out more inside information about the company, but your resume will also get an extra look because you have made a connection with someone who is in a position to move you ahead.

Whereas your skills are an essential component in the hiring decision, employers also expect you to be educated about their business. That's another reason companies are attracted to social media. It allows them to get the word out about who they are—and, as a result, they can make better matches with future employees. Keith McIlvaine, a former Unisys global social media recruitment lead, said, "[Social media] helps us to paint that picture of our solutions, such as cloud computing and security applications. All those variables are important, so when a candidate comes in to interview, the recruiter is sending them to these tabs to look at the Unisys history in Facebook. [They] should go to Facebook and look at the cloud computing or go to YouTube and look at our cloud computing theories. This is going to be important at the interview and it just gives candidates a nice background on what Unisys is doing and it will help you speak more about it and understand it. It's that type of education that social media is so good at."[6]

Besides making you look good at a job interview, how does all this information help you make an informed decision about working for a particular company? Social media is an excellent venue for discovering what a company's culture is all about. In Chapter 1, we spoke about your personal brand and the impression it creates about you. Now it's your turn to look at a company's brand. PPG's Shannon Pelissero said, "Companies need to leverage themselves as an employer of choice. For a candidate that is the impression they have of you. I am very big on first impressions, especially as a recruiter. When you are at a recruitment fair, or when someone comes into your company for an interview, or even when someone first sees your job posting, that's the impression they have of your company. I think an extension of that is the company needs to be out there in the social media space. It's not going away and I think it's here to stay. And I think it shows potential candidates that you are willing to embrace change, you are open to new ideas, which is important to a lot of candidates. It's important to me."[7]

In addition, listen to what the media is saying about your targeted company. As Paul Marchand recommended, set up a Google Alert. Go to *www.google.com/alerts* and monitor the company in the following ways: "as it happens," once a day, or on a weekly basis. Depending on how often you want to receive information, Google will send you a news item relating to the company. Read everything about the prospective employer, so that when you have the face-to-face, your responses to the hiring manager's questions will be informed. It won't go over well if you go into an interview and you don't know that the company just acquired a major supplier of fiber optics or that a new CEO has just been installed. Again, this kind of attention to detail will tell the employer that you are interested specifically in that company and you are, as PepsiCo's Paul Marchand added, "the right candidate, at the right time, for the right needs."[8]

The face-to-face

Think of the job interview as though you are preparing for a test. During your fact-finding mission, you have gathered a lot more information than you can possibly regurgitate during a typical interview, but that's okay. All of this research has prepared you to make a good decision—an important decision that will dramatically affect your life for the next several years. As Google's Sean Splaine said, "I tell people that finding a job is the hardest job you will ever have. It's a full-time job and you need to be proactive about it."[9] As much as you would like to wrap up the job hunt shebang and put it behind you, you still have a few more bases to cover.

So what's next? Review your resume and make about five hard copies of it to bring to the interview. This is the resume that has all the beautiful formatting in place—not your plaintext sample that you sent via the ATS. If you tweaked your resume for this specific job, make sure you have nailed down every detail to memory—and you bring the correct resume, not the one you sent to the other employer last week.

Your resume will likely form the basis of the initial face-to-face conversation, and there's also a good chance, according to Pitney Bowes' Laura Terenzi Khaleel, that "it may not be viewed fully and completely until somebody gets to an interview."[10] HR people are busy. Maybe they are doing a lot of prescreening and your resume was matched up to the open position by a keyword search; maybe only snippets of your resume were quickly scanned by human eyes. Now that you are coming in for the face-to-face, though, you can be fairly certain a human being is looking at the complete CV—A to Z. You should know what's on your resume. Believe it or not, sometimes applicants are a little too vague about resume specifics.

A few Fortune 500 hiring managers also mentioned that they often view the LinkedIn profile prior to meeting with a prospective employee. That's why you want that profile to be crisp, clear and current—emphasizing your top qualifications and the skills you want to bring forward to your next job. CIGNA's Eric Kaulfuss said, "You can pick up a lot of keywords from the profile itself. It almost acts as a resume. Using a bunch of ways to describe your role over and over again is probably a good strategy to follow."[11] That's one of the reasons why all your communication with a prospective employer— whether it is a cover letter, an e-mail, a profile on LinkedIn, a resume, during the face-to-face—needs to be professional, succinct, and accurate. You are being evaluated on *all* of it. Do not let last-minute carelessness ruin an opportunity.

Hiring managers may be viewing your resume on LinkedIn; reviewing your blog and other information that may be out there on the Web. When preparing for your interview it is not only important to think about what you've done, but, to take the time to think about how you've accomplished all that you've done and the steps that you've taken to get there. Erik Qualman, author of *Socialnomics*, told us, "Once you are in the interview, it is no longer about 'tell me your story' it is about 'show me your story.' The Internet provides employers the ability to gather information from you online, so it is important to go into the interview prepared to provide examples of how you've achieved the results highlighted in your resume. It is a more quantifiable approach. Don't be surprised to have an interviewer turn their computer monitor toward you and say, 'Show me this blog you created that helped increase traffic 140 percent. Walk me through how you optimized this blog for search engines.' This is show versus tell."[12]

The reason five hard copies of your resume should be in your briefcase when you show up for the face-to-face is that, if you get past the HR gatekeeper (who will fill you in on the particulars of the job and speak to you about your salary range, if that wasn't discussed earlier in a prescreening telephone interview or as part of the application process on the ATS), there's a chance you will speak to other individuals during the day—possibly the person you will be directly reporting to or his or her superior as well as an assortment of other key managers.

Ask the person who schedules the appointment what you can expect the day of your interview and how much time you should allow. You can do that during your telephone conversation or through an e-mail, if that is how that person made initial contact with you. The more you know about what to expect, the better. You don't want to have to rush through the interview because you have an important meeting at your current company at 1 p.m. And asking relevant questions about the process attests to your professionalism.

Although a good part of a recruiter's job is disqualifying candidates, if you are asked to come in for a face-to-face, most employers want you to succeed. You are probably one of five gold nuggets that they have prospected. Narrowing the applicant pool and finding you are labor-intensive initiatives. Martin Cepeda, a senior recruiter at a Fortune 500 healthcare company, said that some recruiters will even prepare you for the interview: "I've worked at companies that do mock interviews and practice with [candidates] before their actual interview to get them ready for the interview. So they are pretty much setting them up for success to help them feel more comfortable so that their true competencies come through during the interview."[13]

The big day

By the time your interview rolls around, employers have a fair amount of information about you already—especially now that social media has made access so easy. Now the company wants to see if you can think on your feet. Every interview is give-and-take—and your questions are just important as your answers—so make sure you listen carefully, so you can respond appropriately and follow up on any new information that arises during the interview. What is an employer interested in knowing about you—that they don't know already—on the big day?

Although they have probably seen a photo of you already—thanks to LinkedIn or other social venues—an employer does want to see that you are "presentable." Wear the best shoes you can afford (and, if applicable, be sure your pocketbook and/or briefcase are high quality as well) and dress in business attire—an outfit, preferably a suit, that fits you, is clean, and is on the conservative side. Business attire nowadays varies (some companies prefer casual dress), but you are trying to make a good impression, so it is perfectly reasonable to ask the person who arranges the interview if you would be overdressed if you showed up in a suit.

Basically you want to make the statement that you are well-groomed, aware of protocol, and that this interview means something to you and you are willing to go out of your way to make a good impression. Have a positive mindset. Also take into account that you are being evaluated on whether you would work well with your future group, so avoid gum-chewing (although a breath mint beforehand isn't a bad idea), wear deodorant, and do not smell of smoke. Make sure any lingering pieces of salad are not stuck in your teeth, hair and nails are clean and/or manicured, and you're not wearing too much perfume or cologne. Greet everyone you meet—from the receptionist to the hiring manager—in a positive manner. Look like you're happy to be there. Be on time, but arrive no more than five minutes ahead of schedule. These are the basics, but so many have been disqualified on these simple prerequisites.

You also need to remember to look people in the eye when you shake their hands, and follow their lead when you sit down for the interview. Never speak negatively about a former employer. And small talk should also be non-inflammatory—even if it's about the weather or the latest Bronco game. Politely decline a cup of coffee and instead stay focused on the task at hand. It's all right to be nervous, but try not to be on the verge of a breakdown. Deep breathing for five minutes before the interview will calm the nerves. Try Dr. Weil's stress-buster: inhaling through the nose on the count of 4, holding the breath to the count of 7, then exhaling forcefully through the mouth on the count of 8. It's an excellent method for taking away the jitters and quelling the racing mind.

After these preliminaries, it's all about your work—past, present, and future—and your communication skills. Cameron's Megan Dick said, "We look for a certain level of experience before we consider an employee, but when it comes to meeting that person and interviewing them, there are many factors that go into it other than just what kind of experience they have and how long they've been working. We also look at who's going to come in and be a really good fit for the company and who's got something to offer."[14]

By now it should be clear to you what you have to offer a new company—remember you are the solution to the employer's problem and your extensive research has given you some insight into what the solution is—but you still need to listen carefully to exactly what is being said at the face-to-face. Perhaps the emphasis has shifted. Anything can happen in a week. Pay attention to this shift. Rebecca Shafir, author of *The Zen of Listening,* calls this "critical listening." In her book, she says, "In our information-laden world, we simply do not have the time to listen to everything that comes our way, so we have to make decisions between listening to things we *should* hear and what we *want* to hear."[15] If you assumed you were going to spend most of your work day at the new job on systems architecture and the primary topic of conversation during the interview is software engineering, then you need to make an adjustment during the interview—provided you are still interested—and ask questions regarding software engineering and not systems architecture. Respond to what is actually being said.

Time and again, Fortune 500 hiring professionals said the face-to-face is crucial when making a hiring decision. They want to know how you work—on projects, with others, and with your superiors and direct reports. Those topics—and how you communicate them—are what matter. When Hewlett-Packard's Kathy Hooson evaluates a candidate she wants to know "what the person has been doing, how they have progressed through their career, the activities they are involved with in the business world."[16] And Ian Decker, from MetLife, said, "We're really looking at a candidate's skills and job stability, whether they were at a company for a long time. There are a lot of factors that play into it."[17] UPS's Dan McMackin said, "The face-to-face works wonders. I don't want to sound old-fashioned, versus this new way of finding people, but we've been doing the [face-to-face] for 103 years and it's proven pretty valid. We have employment people in every location in the country who are trained professionally.... We talk about promotion from within, that's a cultural thing here. It's a matter of bench strength.... [Candidates] have to be willing to learn our job, learn our culture, and if they perform well, then they are going to be promoted. The opportunity is there. They have to show the initiative and willingness to do it."[18]

From the preceding comments you can assume that the "factors" that go into a hiring decision are as varied as the employers, but you still need to be on your best game during the interview. Basically how well the job interview goes depends on how you answer the employer's questions as well as what kind of questions you ask. Strive for a 50-50 exchange of information between employer and future employee. Keep focused on *the work you want to do.*

The employer might ask you the following questions:

- What made you choose your career?
- Where do you see yourself two years from now?
- What is your definition of an ideal job?
- Why did you major in [chemistry, history, marketing, communications, fill in blank]?
- What would your former employer say were your strengths?
- Why are you leaving your current position?
- Why do you want this job at this company?
- What would your former employer say was your weakness?
- What competencies would you like us to help you develop?
- Why do you want this particular job at this particular company?
- How did you accomplish this achievement you have highlighted on your resume? (Remember, it is not just about 'Tell me your story," but "show me your story.")

Think about how you would answer these questions before you show up for the face-to-face. You don't want to sound as though you memorized a script, but generally just mulling these topics over beforehand will give you a sense of how to respond to the employer's specific questions. You can also avert many of those language tics—*uh, you know, like*—when you have a good sense of what you plan to say. If you want to be even more specific, take another look at the job posting to which you responded. It contains a ton of information about the work you will be expected to do. Draw up a list of questions based solely on the job description, then trot those questions out during the interview if this information isn't already offered. And, by all means, be true to yourself because the fit has to work both ways. Don't pretend you like HTML when you hate it. Don't fudge your distaste for data entry if that's a big part of the new job. Don't say you enjoy seeing the sun come up and you wouldn't mind the early shift when you repeatedly drag yourself out of bed at 8:30 a.m. every work day. And don't say you are willing to travel or relocate if you are glued to your hometown.

Always consider how the question that is being asked relates to what you did and what you want to be doing in the future. Stan Weeks said, "We base our hiring on our interview and our face-to-face relationship with that candidate and what that person brings to the table with regard to their skill set."[19] Talk in depth about the skills you have already acquired that will help you to move easily into the next position. Kellogg's Carolyn Rice said, "I was working in the automotive industry for 13 years, but I knew many of my skills were very transferable to other industries." If you are moving to another industry, think about your transferable skills, too. And don't be averse to contract work. Rice said, "One of my favorite suggestions for finding a new job is through independent contract work. In the automotive industry, 30 percent of our hires came from temporary workers. We got a good look at the person and we could see what they could do. It's a great way to gain entry into a company."[20]

Ask and you shall receive

When we mentioned earlier in the chapter that you need to ask questions, too, we were not referring to questions like, "How much does this job pay?" You don't initiate this conversation unless the hiring manager does it first. Same goes for "How much time do I get off?" and "What kind of benefits does this place offer?" That information will be readily provided—if the HR person thinks you are a viable candidate. Although these aspects are of prime importance to you, the company is interested in what you can do for them first and foremost.

Instead, ask questions directly related to the position being offered, such as:

- Can you give me an idea of what you see me doing on a day-to-day basis?
- Who will I be reporting to?
- What kind of outside training do you provide to heighten skills and teach new knowledge?
- Is this position being created or am I replacing someone? Why did that person leave?
- Can you identify the steps I must take to maximize my success at this company?
- What is the normal interval before someone in my position is considered for promotion?
- What are some of the most critical goals the department needs to achieve in the next six months?
- What problems do you anticipate I will face in my new role?
- How often will you assess my performance?
- Can you tell me about your corporate culture and what it takes to succeed in this organization?
- Will I be expected to work on existing campaigns or will I be initiating some of my own?
- Can you give me an approximate timeframe on how long it will take you to fill this position? If my qualifications fit the job, how long will it take before I hear from you?

Many of these questions should be directed at the appropriate person—the one who can provide detailed answers and explain what is involved in performing well in your future position. Do not ask a question for the sake of asking. Instead gauge who is the best person to answer your question. That will change depending on how deep you go into the company. You want to create a rapport with the person you are speaking to—the click has to happen—so lobbing unnecessary questions at people who are ill equipped to answer them won't further your cause. Pace yourself. Throw-away questions—things you should know from your research prior to the interview—are not a good idea. Instead take mental notes of the information provided by the hiring managers that day, and then follow up with questions directly related to what you heard at the interview.

The other kind of follow-up

You can score a lot of points by following the fast break down the court. You can also score a lot of points when you consistently follow up while job hunting. In earlier chapters we talked about seizing opportunities to make inroads into a company by contacting a recruiter you meet, for instance, at a career fair. CIGNA's Eric Kaulfuss went even further when he made this suggestion:

> If you go to a company Website or a job posting site, and you have this LinkedIn bar up there, it will tell you who you know or who's in your network at this company. My thought is that you zero in on the HR people, especially the recruiters. And, having applied [via the company career site], you say, "Hey, I just want to let you know I applied to this job. I'm connected to you through LinkedIn. If you wouldn't mind introducing me to whomever the recruiter is." I found that to be a very effective approach. It shows some initiative. It shows some research. It shows some judgment. And those are the types of things we are looking for when we hire people anyway. We want them to take initiative. We want them to have good judgment. We want them to be polite.[21]

This also applies to the interview. Every person you meet when you interview at a company should receive a thank-you note afterward. Not only does it imply you are still interested in the job after speaking with them, but it also shows that you are appreciative of their time and effort. This means, of course, that you have everyone's name or business card, so you can connect with them yet again after the interview.

Sometimes interviews are so nerve-wracking that you forget names and faces and whatnot. That's not an excuse for not sending a note of gratitude. If you have drawn a complete blank, simply call up the receptionist at the company where you interviewed and ask for the information you need. She may not know everyone you met with that day, but she can certainly provide you with the contact information for the HR generalist or manager. Of course, a better scenario is that you jot down some notes or gather business cards while you are interviewing with each individual. This attention to detail exhibits a certain level of professionalism as well as composure.

You may be wondering if it's appropriate to send an e-mail in lieu of a note. Activision's Lissa Freed said, "Every once in a while you get a handwritten thank-you card after the interview. The handwritten card is nice because it is a reminder that people still do this, but e-mails get forwarded and archived and what have you, so you are probably better off sending an e-mail."[22] MGM's Michael Peltyn said, "Another thing we make a mental note of is a thank-you correspondence. We like that. It actually registers with the hiring managers when someone takes the time. It can be as simple as a three-line e-mail. Really, it doesn't have to be an elaborate form of communication—just thanking the hiring manage for their time; reiterating interest in the job and company. I've seen that prove to be a difference-maker. The best thing you can do, especially in our industry, is send a handwritten note. A handwritten card, mailed, really shows the most attention to detail, but I would say at a minimum, an e-mail or letter or something to acknowledge the interview."[23] It's up to you which method you prefer, but look at the thank-you note as another opportunity to connect. Besides expressing appreciation for their time and boosting your interest in the position, feel free to write a line or two about the company or job that you may have neglected to mention while you were speaking to the hiring managers that day.

How long will it take to hear about whether you have the job or not? It all depends on how critical the position is. CIGNA's Eric Kaulfuss said, "From the first point where we usually connect with a person to the point where we make an offer, it takes about 45 days. We try to build up an opportunistic pipeline, so that helps a lot. That's the average. But if you're relocating people and flying them into a different location, then obviously it's going to take more time."[24] But just so you know, some other Fortune 500 professionals said it takes anywhere from three to six months—from start to finish—to bring a new employee onboard.

Once you have interviewed, you may be eager to hear right away, but that may not happen. A background check usually takes three to five days, and it may be days or even weeks afterward before someone gets back to you regarding the job. While it's all right to check in—in fact, why not ask the employer how often you should do so. EdisonLearning's Brett Goodman said, "It's very important to follow up. When a person contacts me two weeks later to ask if I received the materials, I know that person is serious about wanting to work at my company. Follow-up is crucial, but there's also a fine line between persistence and being a nudge."[25]

The best offer

If you do get an offer, spend some time considering it before responding with an affirmative or negative. Certainly every company will give you 24 hours; most will give you more time. You have to weigh all the pros and cons. You may know what the company is willing to pay you, or occasionally the salary is not determined until the offer is made, which means you can continue negotiations. Be firm, but be reasonable—and, at all times, be professional. PepsiCo's Paul Marchand said, "My wife is a recruiter. We are both in HR. She told me about a candidate this week who they were recruiting for some time. They gave her the offer. They thought she was going to accept. They waited for her response for five days and she declined the job offer—through an e-mail. Do you think my wife is going to remember that name? For sure. Do recruiters and managers get upset when a person doesn't take their job offer? Of course they do. Do you try to rebound with more money or let me hear about your concerns? Are we as competitive as we always are? Absolutely. Despite the economy, if we want somebody, we are all competitive about trying to get that person and we want that person to say yes instead of no. That being said, for her to respond in an e-mail was...majorly unprofessional."[26]

If an employment contract is not offered, you do not have to hide your disappointment, but do remain courteous. Ask to be considered for future positions. If you made it that far in the hiring process, the employer obviously saw something in you that it liked—and you may have another shot at an even better job down the road.

Making hiring decisions is difficult, and most companies value their reputation, so try to be philosophical about it and have faith that something better is in store for you. A good company will appreciate your effort and professionalism. PPG's Shannon Pelissero said, "We've taken the approach that every prospective employee is also a potential customer. So we have to understand that even if we don't select someone as a candidate, we still keep them as a customer."[27] Paul Marchand concurs: "The employment experience is no different than the consumer-brand experience, so if you don't like that product, you are going to tell people about it. Whether the person got the job or not, if he or she had a great candidate experience and we returned that person's e-mail or LinkedIn note and we brought that person in and we talked to him or her and we rolled out the red carpet and that person had a great, Ritz-Carlton-like consumer experience as an applicant, if that person doesn't get the job, my belief is that he or she will say, 'Great company, wasn't the right time/right place for me, but it could be for you.'"[28]

Chapter 10

On Becoming an Employee of Choice

Hyperconnectivity is the next evolution.
—Shally Steckerl
Executive Vice President
Arbita

Let's assume you got the job and now you're thinking it's time to kick back. After all, you just expended tons of energy pulling all these pieces together—you deserve to celebrate. By all means, take a breather and pat yourself on the back for landing the perfect job, but don't forget that networking and leveraging your personal brand are an ongoing commitment. Your network needs to continue to thrive, regardless of the fact that you are now happily employed, and your personal brand needs continual refining, even though you are now relishing your new Herman Miller Aeron chair.

When we reached out to Fortune 500 professionals for *The Web 2.0 Job Finder,* they told us time and again that they approach social media from two vantage points. CSC's Jim Gattuso called it a "two-prong" approach: "One is our ability to present information to candidates and the other is to obtain information in finding candidates."[1] Social media allows companies to position themselves as "employers of choice" by getting the message out about what they value as well as what they have to offer. Companies can enhance their brand inexpensively and in real-time. CIGNA's Kaulfuss said, "I think the ability to share it and get it out there and show your brand off are really key to it—and to do it at relatively low expense. I mean it didn't cost us any money other than time to set up our Facebook site—and we can put out a nice branded advertisement on there for free and it can be shared across the blogosphere for very little."[2] What is so incredible about social networking is that nothing is stopping you from doing this as well. In the Web 2.0 world, you can easily position yourself as an *employee* of choice. You are, after all, the author of this experience, so imagine the possibilities and create the opportunities.

Your "two-prong" approach should be to continually grow your network and keep your personal brand in front of people. How do you do this? By developing a strategy and understanding the networking platform you are using. EA's Cindy Nicola said her company gets so much traction from Facebook's InsideEA because the company understands its audience ("They love exclusive information" and "fun"—"Games are what we do") as well as how best to showcase its brand (Facebook for gamers). This integrated mindset drives EA's Facebook campaign: "InsideEA allows us to engage on three distinct platforms: games, people and opportunities," but EA also recognizes that there has to be a "stronger convergence between PR and product marketing teams...because there is a very fine line between future hires and consumers."[3]

That's what is happening in social. Even though you joke with your friends and family on Facebook and stiffen up considerably on LinkedIn, you're probably noticing that the fine lines are getting blurry—or maybe blended is a better word. Nicola said, "More than 50 percent of my Facebook friends are actually colleagues and business connections, which by default means I have blended the two. This works at EA because (A) we make video games and social media is at the heart of what we do, and (B) one of our core leadership values is 'Be human first—bring your whole self to work,' so for EA, it works."[4] This core value of being "human first" might help your social strategy too.

If you are serious about developing a personal brand, maybe what really has to happen is for you to develop a voice that is appropriate for a blended audience. Instead of talking in compartmentalized tongues, use a language that is conversational, friendly and authentic in all your online communication. Bridge the big disconnect between "I plan to implement private equity and debt investment programs to raise equity capital" and "I need a couple bucks to invest in some hot property." Be simple and be clear—in all your communication. Corp-speak is typically not friendly. That doesn't mean you can't still talk about the wavelength of a blue laser or the embedded data of the Semantic Web, but strive to do so in plain English. Consider your audience. Consider your platform. You want your audience to understand and you want them to engage—because when they do, you'll learn more and your network will become more robust. Of course, if you want to be less than upfront, obfuscate, and then obfuscate some more. No one will want to read what you've written, which might be the whole point anyhow, and you will be left to your own devices—at least until the Feds catch on.

The wince factor

One of the riskier aspects of social networking, for companies as well as individuals, is that with all this engagement it's difficult to control content. Many companies and newcomers often shy away from social media precisely because of this. When we were doing our research for *The Web 2.0 Job Finder,* we noticed on Newell Rubbermaid's Facebook page that a job applicant posted that no one had gotten back to her yet and a consumer complained he was missing bolts in the package that arrived from the company that day. We asked Mike Rickheim about this and he said,

The primary purpose of our presence [on Facebook] today is related to educating our potential employment base about the opportunities here. We keep a very close eye on this and make sure we're getting back to the candidates who say, 'Hey, I haven't heard anything. I'm looking for an update.' We'll direct them to our applicant tracking system, share details about our process, and let them know that if they aren't a great fit for a particular role we'll keep them in mind for other things. We're also seeing that social media sites are a popular avenue for somebody looking for customer service assistance. While we obviously prefer to keep the content [on Facebook] as focused and positive as possible, we recognize we are dealing with human nature and people will likely try many communication options in an effort to get answers to their customer service questions quickly. This includes social media.[5]

There's that word again: *human.* If you've spent any time on Facebook, you probably know that word all too well yourself. (We know we've had our own fair share of Facebook winces.) But that's the thing about social networking, it's all about keeping it real and how you handle it—calmly, rationally, patiently (we hope). "One thing we love about social media is the opportunity to quickly identify whether the consumer has a question or concern with a product," Rickheim continued. In the case of my team, we are focused on recruiting talent to Newell Rubbermaid, so what we're doing with the Facebook page is specific to recruiting, but customer service handles brand or product inquiries to make sure that consumers get the help they need. It's just a matter of getting them to the right person to help them with their concerns as quickly as possible."[6]

Arbita's Shally Steckerl predicted that the conversations on social networks will increasingly become "richer, faster, deeper" because "it is going to be one-to-one, one-to-many, many-to-one, that matrix, instead of the top-down matrix."[7] Which means, with all this transparency, it's going to be more difficult for companies (or even individuals) to be unresponsive, impersonal, inhuman, unless they don't care about their customers or audience. Dictating from the top down certainly isn't going to increase the fan base. To grow a network, you need to be human, you need to be decent, you need to be responsive—online and offline.

In his book, *Marketing to the Social Web,* Larry Weber said, "... the social Web isn't just a channel or another medium for marketing messages. In effect, it's becoming the closest thing to physical life. This is very important because, whether you're a small company with a chain of restaurants or a giant corporation with a global presence, you're going to have to start talking to customers and prospects as if they were with you in the room."[8] We mentioned earlier that social media can be compared to a big Thanksgiving dinner. There are hundreds of millions of players in social media, and some, like the in-law from Boston, are just waiting for you to screw up, but look at it as an opportunity to self-correct rather than as a reason not to participate.

In 1964, Marshall McLuhan said, "Under electric technology the entire business of man becomes learning and knowing. In terms of what we still consider an 'economy' (the Greek word for a household), this means that forms of employment become 'paid learning,' and all forms of wealth result from the movement of information."[9] Social media is a great reminder that we are all connected in some way or other. Maybe that's what has been forgotten in our current economy; that we are all part of a big household. It's time for the conversation to become more real and meaningful. Real growth will not occur otherwise.

Fortunately the dialogue is underway in the 2.0 world. The conversations are spirited. The collaboration is enthusiastic and creative. That's all a good thing. You just need to remember not to dig in your heels and say, "I'm sick of change. Why can't everything stay the same?" Instead, remain open, make the most of it, continue to learn, learn, learn—move that information! We hope you get rich in the process (both intellectually and financially!).

Investigate like Sherlock

Never before has the job seeker had so much access to the marketplace—as well as the companies that are hiring. Always investigate what's out there, regardless of whether you are gainfully employed or not. As Kellogg's Rice said, "Everyone should realize that in this environment nothing is necessarily permanent. As I said before, don't rely on your network just when you need to find a new job. Networking should be ongoing."[10] In addition, it is always important to know your market value, so engaging in conversations about your profession is extremely valuable. In 2009 Facebook had more than 1.4 million business Pages—where companies extol their brand as well as their opportunities.[11] Nowadays it is easy to do job-finding research. And if your eyes are tired from reading all day, watch some video on YouTube. Lisa Beauclaire said, "Our marketing department has really been utilizing YouTube from the standpoint of getting more consumer education out there about our products, but we're also creating AmFam Careers as a segment of American Family Insurance's YouTube Channel."[12] Ryder's Kirk Imhof said:

> From a candidate's perspective, there are a number of avenues you can take to get to know a company better. More and more, companies are using employer branding to reflect their cultures, environments, and offerings in a way that attracts candidates. That brand then becomes a message used in marketing their opportunities. With Ryder, our employer brand is truthful. It's based on research, it's based on what our employees think of us, and it's based on what our marketplace thinks of us. It's based on what candidate pools that have been attracted to both us and to our competitors think of us. We have taken that information and from it we have crafted our employer value proposition or employer brand, so the brand itself reflects who we are. We try to incorporate our brand messaging in all our employment advertising. Paying attention to that messaging is one way to get to know us—and it's a very reliable way to get to know who we are and the type of organization we are.[13]

Companies want their brands to be accurate portrayals of what they stand for. It's important in the digital world that you too are accountable and reliable. Let's say you notice a sales director position is up for grabs at a favorite company. Maybe you don't have the skills or experience just yet. The good news is that you have investigated and now know what's required—you can make a decision to develop those skills—and go back to that company when you're ready. You don't have to remain in the dark about the job market any longer; the digital marketplace spells out in black and white what's required to be successful in every field and industry.

While looking for a job, it's a good idea to always cast yourself in the best light, but don't overinflate your abilities. An honest assessment will move you closer to your goal than hype and hoopla. Some individuals—and even companies—learn this lesson the hard way.

The Global Language Monitor recently announced that the top word for 2010 was *spillcam*[14]—the live video that went viral during the Gulf of Mexico offshore oil spill. BP initially underestimated the havoc the largest oil spill in U.S. history wreaked. Viral footage and outrage on Twitter and Facebook changed the company's tune—quickly. "A more proactive stance on social media sites might have curbed the negative sentiment,"[15] said Douglas MacMillan in a *Bloomberg Businessweek* article. The digital world doesn't have much patience for the "no comment" antics of arrogance. Honesty is important and the lack of it will get you into trouble. Remember Bill Clinton, "I didn't inhale," versus Barack Obama, "When I was a kid, I inhaled." Social media will hold you accountable, too, so stick to the truth.

When you are investigating present and future options, don't leave any stones unturned. In *The Web 2.0 Job Finder,* our discussion was limited to certain social sites—namely LinkedIn, Facebook, YouTube, and Twitter—primarily because our participants told us that when they recruit they go to where applicants and customers flock "en masse." This doesn't mean you shouldn't branch out and do your own exploring. Find out where engineers or accountants or copy editors or marketing professionals gather online. Look at the job boards that are specific to your profession. Activision's Lissa Freed said, "What we have found is a big source of recruiting for us is via the industry sites. So in our case, Gamasutra, Gamedeveloper, those kinds of sites, we like to tap into the industry trade sites—that are core to the business—and hang out."[16] Heather McBride-Morse thinks it's important to supplement your online networking with more traditional methods as well. She said, "I have become involved in my local HR chapter, so there are chapters for every industry and profession. Get involved in those. When you get a business card, go type that person's name—the next day, in fact—into LinkedIn. Say, 'Great meeting you last night. I just wanted to add you to my contacts.'"[17] We got this message from several Fortune 500 HR professionals—use every tool in your toolbox when networking, whether it's traditional or social. But stay organized. Integrate both approaches without scattering your energies in every direction.

The dynamics of social media

The Web 2.0 Job Finder has emphasized throughout that it's essential to understand the platform of whatever social networking site you use. Without a doubt, it's important to ask what makes a particular site unique, what kind of ROI can you expect, who is the audience? You have to feel your way around to get a sense of how the site operates. But remember, social media is highly sensitive to change. Users often direct which way the platform will go. Pitney Bowes' Khaleel said:

> Facebook is a major blend between personal and business conversations, whereas LinkedIn tends to be more exclusive. I won't say 100-percent exclusive, but much more tilted toward professional networking conversation. Yes, Facebook is a mixture. And I do think folks are utilizing it to network about jobs. Having said that, social media is changing dramatically and drastically and so it would be impossible for me to predict, even several months from now, where several of these medias are headed. Twitter, for example, is big and it's

hot and it's out there and you have to utilize it as an employer for getting word out about jobs, but in terms of interaction, I don't know. There's a lot of controversy about utilizing Twitter. Some people love it. Some people hate it. It's changing so dramatically.[18]

Khaleel doesn't see any real "interaction," which makes sense, because there's really not a whole lot of dialogue going on (although you can reply to individual tweets), but Twitter is an excellent vehicle to build a brand or position yourself as an expert. For example, plug in the word *Linux* in the search bar. We just did and we found a tip from LinuxPower on how to sync an iPad to Linux (just follow the link provided in the tweet). If LinuxPower's suggestion works without a hitch, the tweeter might get a "follow." If LinuxPower comes up with more solutions—or is just plain interesting—his/her following will grow, as will his/her brand.

Twitter resembles a stream-of-consciousness brain—one unrelated thought after another—but it's streaming in real time, along with the other 180 million minds on Twitter. And there's no better way to take the pulse of a situation, a company, a controversy, a catastrophe. What's going on at the White House? What's going on at IBM? What's going on with Julian Assange? It's all there once you plug it into the search bar. Looking for a job? Plug in a location or a company. That's all there too. "I think social media provides job seekers with another source of information and I think one of the reasons everyone loves social media is that it enables everyone to have their voice heard. You can go to a corporate Website and it's very stale—with clip art...I think social media feels more real and genuine. They can see the comments people posted. It makes more of an impact actually than a corporate Website does,"[19] said PPG's Shannon Pelissero.

It can be difficult sometimes to wrap your arms around social media precisely because it is so "real" and dynamic—it doesn't stand still—but that can also be part of its appeal because it mirrors how human beings behave. We are constantly moving, constantly forming new alliances, constantly sharing information, constantly collaborating. Lisa

Beauclaire said, "And that's what is wonderful about social media—that people can join your community, even if there's not an opening at a given time. It's a little different than the typical applicant tracking system, which is much more effective if there is an opening at the time you are talking to them and they are posting their resume."[20] Social media is not mechanistic; it's responsive.

And social media is not static, but sometimes it feels that way when you first get started. Stryker's Laurie Byrne said the biggest leap in social media is "the first part of testing the water is one-way communication. Once you have a level of comfort and you're actually positioned and set up so you can respond appropriately and within a decent timeframe and manage how you respond, then I think you're willing to take Step 2, which is actually the 2.0 or more-than-2-way leap. That's really the biggest leap. The first one is showing up at all and then...the second one is allowing that dialogue to occur."[21] Getting the dialogue to move along takes time and you have to be willing to engage regularly. Check in, share, collaborate. Have something to offer—and be willing to receive. As James Suroweicki said, "For me, one of the key lessons of *The Wisdom of Crowds* is that we don't always know where good information is. That's why, in general, it's smarter to cast as wide a net as possible, rather than wasting time figuring out who should be in the group and who should not."[22]

Your future and its future

If you have spent any time with teenagers lately, you are bound to have noticed that you don't have their full attention. There's this little doodad in their pockets competing for attention—they're looking at you, then they're looking at their pockets. It's killing them—looking at you. If you don't scowl, they will actually pull the doodad out and suddenly forget you ever existed. You used to get offended. Now you're used to it. The cell phone rules. "Allison Miller, 14, sends and receives 27,000 texts in a month, her fingers clicking at a blistering pace as she carries on as many as seven text conversations at a time. She texts between classes, at the moment soccer practice ends, while being driven to and from school and, often, while studying,"[23] said Matt Richtel in "Growing Up Digital—Wired for Distraction." You might not want to hear this, but our future is...constant connection.

In November 2010, the unemployment rate jumped to 9.8 percent—with nearly 15 million Americans out of work and nearly 6.3 million unemployed for the long term. It's been a rough few years. We could blame the Quants on Wall Street, those math whizzes who believed that Wall Street was a numbers game having nothing to do with the quality or strength of American business.[24] Or we could blame the politicians who stuck their head in the sand as banks showered money on the already over-leveraged. We could blame a lot of people actually, but that's not going to get us anywhere. The world is changing. Are we paying attention? Are we making the necessary adjustments? Are we retraining and retooling?

Chris Anderson, *Wired* magazine's editor and author of *The Long Tail,* talks about how fiber optics allowed India's $2-a-minute phone call in 1990 to become a 7-cents-a-minute phone call a few years later. A technological advance, fourth-generation fiber optics, changed everything, including the workplace. While fiber optics weren't free, it allowed communication to become cheap. Anderson calls *free* "Silicon Valley's gift to the world,"[25] even though many Americans paid a hefty price for this gift. Businesses no longer had to pay American workers what someone in China or India could do for half the cost. Outsourcing made perfect financial sense. That is the new reality. James O'Toole and Edward E. Lawler said, in *The New American Workplace,* "Realistically, in the future more workers in more companies are likely to lose jobs as their tasks are moved offshore or automated."[26]

During the most recent recession, a devastating one to be sure, businesses learned how to do more with less. They will rehire—many Fortune 500 companies said the freeze is thawing—but probably not as robustly as they did prior to the 2007 meltdown. That means you have to be prepared. You have to take charge of your future. How? Retrain or brush up your skills so you can shift to a more sustainable business; create your own business; work for a start-up; change careers; innovate. Like the best businesses, be flexible and nimble. Or—what *The Web 2.0 Job Finder* is really all about—you could make sure you are continually learning new skills and marketing them appropriately.

Ron Gosdeck, the vice president of Global Recruiting at Unisys, said, "Apple is changing the world with technology, with things like the iPad and the iPhone. The iPad is a device that is not a PC, but it's wifi-capable, Internet-capable—all those things. We actually have an operation in the Midwest where we're going to give all the employees iPads to work from. We want them to be global, we want them to be current, we want them to be flexible. With the cloud you don't need to have PCs and databases because you can work out of the cloud—doing data or doing whatever it is you need to do."[27] Granted, Unisys is a Fortune 500 tech company, so you would expect it to be ahead of the crowd on mobility, but if you do not plan to run out right now to buy an iPad, you should at least know Gosdeck is not referring to the weather when he talks about the cloud. In this marketplace, you too need to stay "current" and "flexible."

When Michael Peltyn had to hire 170,000 people for MGM Resorts International in the course of a year, he recognized that social media played a significant role in hiring. He said, "Yes, it is obviously the trend, the technology trend. The younger generations are very adept and proficient and we had to brainstorm about the best way to reach that audience. Social media really played a big role in that."[28] When we began writing *The Web 2.0 Job Finder*, our goal was to encourage job seekers to incorporate social networking into their hunting strategy while keeping an eye on best practices at Fortune 500 companies. There are so many trends that happen and don't warrant a book, but as SAIC's David McMichael, assistant vice president and manager of Staffing Strategies and Programs, said, "I'm hopeful that the book will help people come to the realization that [social media] is here to stay."[29] After speaking with our experts it became evident that social was bigger than we initially imagined. In fact, some of the Fortune 500 participants didn't want to talk about Web 2.0; instead they wanted to discuss Web 3.0. Lisa Beauclaire, of American Family Insurance, said, "I think we're going to see a lot more of Twitter in the future because of all the mobile apps. Where mobile technology is now, I don't think many people are looking for jobs via mobile, but give it two years. And that's where I heard about Web 3.0. And if mobile takes off, and I think it will, Twitter will be important."[30]

Social media is being embraced by both large and small business, but, as we already mentioned, they are definitely still exploring Many participants, like Hewlett-Packard's Debbie Mathew, saw social as "a network of pre-building, before you need a job,"[31] and still others were more assertive when it comes to social networking. PepsiCo's Paul Marchand said:

> This is a good topic for me. I manage a team of 80 to 90 recruiters globally. Recruiter's savvy is at an all-time high. They are much more technology savvy than they ever have been in the past. They get information quickly. They deliver information quickly. They use any means that they need to and can. I think that is going to affect us in several ways:
>
> 1. **Sourcing Talent.** I absolutely think, and even I do this, with my limited 41-year-old, user capability of my recruiting job, I will absolutely look and try to find people with no information other than what I find on the Web, so if I have to fill a Chief Marketing Officer, Quaker Brand, Gatorade Brand, or a head of sales, I will absolutely go and target certain companies. I will look at conferences—at the attendees and speakers. I will check out 40 Under 40 lists. I will get some lead names and start generating names off of those names. I will use LinkedIn. I will develop, if you are talking about sourcing, very quickly a short list of potential calls I can make. In the past, that was much harder and much more challenging and you would have to go outside to a search partner or a research firm and say "Get me some of that." That information is much more accessible and now we are at a much more level playing field with those firms.

2. **Ability to get names/referrals from either internal execu-
    tives or from research firms** and then do a lot of legwork
    that we would have to rely upon deep large staff or a third
    party to do. We can now do this by ourselves with a more
    nimble staff because the information and the accessibility
    of the information are pretty real. I can get a profile and a
    candidate on LinkedIn in half a second. Most people have a
    profile on LinkedIn and it would shock you that they do...
    but they do, so that helps you not just with the sourcing
    part, but honing in on "Who do I want to put a call out to,
    and how do I want to get him or her into our company?"
    And get them in for a company interview and to start con-
    sidering them and reaching out to them and whatever. It
    happens and it works. I think what that is going to do is,
    it is going to change the game in terms of how people use
    fee-based sourcing, and that ultimately changes what mat-
    ters. Today, I think there is a world of people who think,
    "I don't have time for a job search." In fact, I am a passive
    job seeker and as long as Spencer Stuart, a big retained
    search firm, has my resume and I know Johnny at Spen-
    cer Stuart, I am fine. The reality is, Spencer Stuart isn't
    getting as many calls to do as many searches as they have
    in the past. In the future, it is the Paul Marchands, who-
    ever, from these corporations who are literally the people
    who are doing the searches. And just having your resume
    with these search firms is not going to be an answer. So
    candidates need to think consciously about what we talked
    about earlier, how do they make sure that their brand is out
    there in some way, how are they networked in some way.
    It has to be done not just when they are actively looking,
    but in a passive way as well. I think it is going to change
    the game. It has changed the way in terms of how recruit-
    ers can work faster, smarter, and easier. It has changed the
    game in terms of getting better and lower fee-based hiring,
    but I think an uptick in quality also, because you can do a

lot of third-party checking and referencing on people and validate that this person jumped 10 times and didn't seem to make it through a performance cycle. They must not be doing something right or this person has gotten a lot of accolades for things that they have done. Well we should talk to the second one, not the first one—knowing that well in advance of an interview, so it helps. On the candidate side, this is going to have an impact because I think the more and more people, the kids are growing up, the students are out there in the universities and they are using all of these social sites and they are using all of these quote unquote individual branding environments. They are not going to be as apt to go to a search firm or rely only on a search firm to get a job. They are going to say, "Hey, I can do this on my own. I can do this with the Pauls." Part of the responsibility is on the candidate community to stay current, stay fresh, stay relevant, but keep it tight and crisp. The responsibility is also on the recruiter community, I mean the corporate recruiter community, which has to have the infrastructure. You've got to have savvy recruiters, you have to have the right technology, and you have to be responsive and collaborative as well. Those who aren't will get blasted on the Internet, I am sure. Thankfully, the stuff that is out there about us is pretty good. We have talked to people like Glass Door and Vault.com about how we continue to help ensure that the message is correct and transparent without obviously influencing people's reviews of our company. It is very transparent now that the employment experience is no different than the consumer brand experience, so if you don't like that product, you are going to tell people about it.[32]

Everyone we interviewed for *The Web 2.0 Job Finder* used LinkedIn to find candidates, but Facebook, Twitter, YouTube and blogs were still up for grabs. Everyone, however, is watching Facebook carefully: "I mean LinkedIn has a lot more joiners every day, but obviously it doesn't have the numbers of Facebook," [33] said Lisa Beauclaire. And Arbita's Shally Steckerl said:

> One [social network] will eventually come up with a feature set that far exceeds the other and there is no barrier to entry right now. LinkedIn thinks it has a barrier for entry. Let me tell you, thinks because it has 80 million members that all of a sudden it has made it. But it doesn't take a lot for people to decide to abandon it, so overcomplicating, making it obtuse, making it slow and not growing its usefulness. Now if LinkedIn continues to grow its usefulness, then it has a shot. You know who is doing that very well, it's Facebook. It's becoming more and more useful—now they have LBS—location-based search. They have blogs. They have photo sharing. [34]

Newell Rubbermaid's Mike Rickheim said:

> I think social networking is a necessary part of any recruiting strategy. It really has become that. I would not have said that a year ago. The trend is such that if we don't realize that it's a necessary avenue today, we're all going to kick ourselves in a year. I had a meeting this morning about how we are going to incorporate text recruiting and text applications into our strategy. Text recruiting seems insane to me right this minute, but we have to get out in front of this right now, before we're playing catch up—in probably six, twelve, eighteen months. We could be on a call in two years and the fact that people are not able to apply via text would seem crazy to us. The recruiting world is changing quickly—and social networking is a big part of this. [35]

While leveraging Twitter and recruiting via mobile messaging seems to have the recruiters intrigued, many are in the early phases of using this technology, but based on sheer volume and possibility of mass adoption, the potential is huge. It's a natural progression. "By the end of 2011, Nielsen expects more Smartphones in the U.S. market than feature phones." [36] Cell phones rule: Everyone has a mobile phone and the smart phone provides many of the capabilities of a computer, such as e-mail and the Internet. As the two devices become more akin, and people start spending more time on their phones than they do on their computers, there's a good chance that in a few years your next opportunity will show up on your telephone. And, another added benefit, telephones are cost-effective, so they are much more inclusive.

Unisys's Abigail Whiffen said, "I think one of the areas that we're talking about right now is we're considering whether a mobile app could assist us with career fairs, where we will walk away with a stack of resumes and CVs, but those applicants have not necessarily signed our waiver or disclaimer of putting their information into our database. If we could be asking them at the career fair to add the Unisys application or if there is a way for them to easily—from their mobile phones—send us their CV in a way that we can get that disclaimer, that would be huge for us, especially in the federal space and potentially in the campus space as well."[37]

Shally Steckerl, executive vice president at Arbita, compared social sites today to the "black and white TV." In his opinion, it's just a matter of time before they morph into a whole new platform. He added that we will not recognize social media as it is today, in fact, many sites "are not all going to make it. The ones that are a convergence of online and social networks, those are the ones that will evolve."[38] Heather McBride-Morse, SPHR/GPHR, manager, Human Resources, Fortune 500 Information Management and Systems company, said she envisions the next generation of social media as "a hub for your virtual life that can then be pushed out to different media. I have one central place that I put all that information in, then it is pushed out to wherever I want it to go."[39]

McBride-Morse's hub idea is interesting and plausible—imagine a one-stop hyper-blend site with bullet-proof privacy screens—but already we are seeing one aspect of social trending toward a norm. CSC's Jim Gattuso thinks social media is currently making an adjustment. "The two platforms are merging and it's going to be an interesting blend as the years go by to see if LinkedIn becomes more social and Facebook becomes more business-oriented."[40] The younger generation already uses social media this way. And, regardless of the pitfalls of blending, on one level, it makes sense. When you spend 40-plus hours a week with people, your colleagues become more than a professional network. They become your friends. As social media grows—becoming a tool in our day-to-day lives—the blend will seem more natural.

SAIC's David McMichael predicted a somewhat different scenario— one that put recruitment and the hiring process squarely on the shoulders of video: "As we look ahead, I bet more communication tools will allow recruiters to almost communicate immediately with candidates—through a shared desktop maybe. Two people are on the phone together and perhaps they even have some kind of video technology on those computers so that they can physically see each other and do an in-person interview in a matter of seconds—a person who is sitting in Paris and another who is sitting in Orlando, Florida. I wouldn't be surprised if that's the direction we go in."[41]

However social media evolves, we can be fairly certain that it will have just as much of an impact on the job market as fiber optics had on outsourcing. But there are some real advantages this time. Authors Barry Libert and Jon Spector (and thousands of other contributors) in *We Are Smarter than Me,* predicted that future workers "will insist that collaboration, much of it remote, replace the traditional authoritarian interactions of manager and employee.... We believe that the corporation as it now exists, with its armies of salaried workers in identical cubicles, will gradually disappear. Instead, there will be virtual communities that will be able to mobilize teams of specialists to take on necessary tasks for customers.[42] Amen to no more cubicles!

So collaborate and innovate. And remember that your resume is a living and breathing document online and should always reflect your most updated information. Constantly build and nourish your network, not just when you are looking for a job—and thank everyone for the help they have given you in landing a new job.

Like any product or company, you need to make sure your online brand is positive, so manage your personal brand as rigorously as a company would. In fact, follow the "principles of brand management" when creating your own personal brand: "Be protected, be easy to pronounce, be easy to remember, be easy to recognize, be easy to know, be easy to translate into all languages in the markets where the brand will be used, attract attention while being attractive, stand out among a group of other brands."[43] And we'll add another principle essential in social media—be real.

In all fairness

Throughout *The Web 2.0 Job Finder* we have cautioned about protecting your reputation. As much as the advantages of social media far outweigh the disadvantages, it was necessary to inform you of the pitfalls—only because individuals continue to make whopping miscalculations online. These things happen. Social media is still evolving. We also recognize that social media will not be embraced by everyone in the near future.

The good news is that most employers are committed to a thorough vetting process. Many substantial factors go into a hiring decision—your online portrayal is only one part of the equation. Unisys's Ron Gosdeck reinforced this idea when he said, "What are the things that drive us to a particular hiring decision? I'm not sure we could even answer that question. It depends on role, it depends on the skill sets we are looking for, it depends on the level of education, it depends on whether it's a government contract; the years of experience, the organizational set, is the individual going to fit into the organization?.... Social media is an avenue for people to get to us, but it hasn't changed the basic, fundamental process. From a corporate governance perspective, we still need to do due diligence."[44]

Social is having a profound impact on hiring, but best practices are still practiced, even in a period of rapid transformation. The challenge—for both employees and employers—is to stay open but make solid decisions on what works and what doesn't. Some companies are already doing this. Having this much access to the particulars of an individual's life made some Fortune 500 employers skeptical of its overall value in terms of hiring decisions.

CSC's Jim Gattuso expressed his concern:

> I think one of the things that lots of Fortune 500 companies are waiting for is some sort of—we want to be aggressive with social media as an emerging platform—but we are also cautious about the legal and privacy issues. I think there's going to be some degree, if not legislation, then certainly some case law that's going to develop over the next few years. Once it becomes clear about where those guidelines will fall and what an employer will and will not be comfortable doing, then I think you're going to see a surge in the use of this. My sense is that a lot of employers right now are being a little cautious about the use of social media as a recruitment tool because those privacy and legal issues have not been totally worked out yet. During the next year or two, as those become clearer (and I hope that it becomes clearer as opposed to even more complex), I think you are going to see a growth in the use of social media as a platform for large employers.[45]

Where does that leave the job seeker? Well, now you know what's at stake. Proceed with gusto now that you know how to work social to your best advantage and adjust your job hunting strategy accordingly. No need to be afraid; get out ahead of the curve. As much as everyone was humbled by the latest economic downturn, it's time to forge ahead. We cannot afford to stay stuck in the sludge. Instead shift your perspective because we have a lot to be grateful for. As Daniel Gardner said, in *The Science of Fear,* "Anyone who has spent an afternoon in a Victorian cemetery knows that gratitude, not fear, should be the defining feeling of our age."[46]

Notes

Introduction

🌐 Pull-out Quotation: Laura Terenzi Khaleel, director, Talent Acquisition Strategies, Pitney Bowes, September 10, 2010.

1. Carolyn Rice, director, Talent Management, Kellogg's, April 5, 2010.
2. Claudia Reilly, national program manager, Recruitment, Avnet, July 29, 2010.
3. David McMichael, assistant vice president and manager, Staffing Strategies and Programs, SAIC, August 18, 2010.
4. Matt Lavery, manager, Corporate Workforce Planning, UPS, August 3, 2010.
5. Holman Jenkins, "Google and the Search for the Future," *Wall Street Journal*, August 14, 2010. *http://online.wsj.com/article/SB10001424052748704901104575423294099527212.html*.
6. Ian Decker, director, Talent Acquisition, MetLife, September 1, 2010.
7. Malcolm Gladwell, *Outliers*, Page 150.
8. David McMichael, August 18, 2010.

Chapter 1

🌐 *Pull-out Quotation:* Mike Rickheim, vice president, Global Talent Acquisition, Newell Rubbermaid, August 30, 2010.

1. John D. Sutter, CNN, "English gets millionth word on Wednesday, site says," *http://articles.cnn.com/2009-06-10/tech/ mil¬lion.words_1_global-language-monitor-millionth-word-new-words?_s=PM:TECH.*

2. Internet World Users by Language: Top 10 Languages, June 30, 2010, *www.internetworldstats.com/stats7.htm.*

3. Tim O'Reilly, "What Is Web 2.0? Design Patterns and Business Models for the Next Generation of Software," *http://oreilly.com/ web2/archive/what-is-web-20.html.*

4. Open source is a movement and a methodology, but simply put, it is free software that can be modified without infringing on a licensing agreement. Open software is owned by the public and the source code can be used for any application.

5. Kirk Imhof, group director, Recruitment, Ryder System, Inc., September 24, 2010.

6. Marshall McLuhan, *Understanding: The Extensions of Man.* See also Federman, M. "What is the Meaning of the Medium is the Message?" (2004, July 23) Retrieved September 15, 2010: *http://individual.utoronto.ca/markfederman/article_mediumist-hemessage.htm.*

7. Keith McIlvaine, a former global social media recruitment lead, Unisys, tweet, September 28, 2010.

8. Kirk Imhof, September 24, 2010.

9. Sarah Needleman, "Internal Hires, Referrals Were Most Hired in 2009," WSJ online. February 25, 2010. Retrieved October 1, 2010: *http://online.wsj.com/article/SB100014240 52748703315 004575073750422889806.html.* Statistics vary on the percentage of jobs filled through networking. In our research we came across the following percentages for how many jobs are filled through networking: 60 percent, 70 percent, and 75 percent.

10. Brian Tracy, *Eat That Frog,* audiobook, BBC Audiobooks America; Unabridged edition, November 8, 2006.

11. "Starbucks Most Popular Brand on Social Networking Sites," Retrieved October 8, 2010: *http://techie-buzz.com/social-networking/starbucks-most-popular-brand-on-social-networking-sites.html.*

12. Charlie Greene, vice president, Trading Systems Development, NYSE Euronext, October 8, 2010.

13. Brett Goodman, recruiter, EdisonLearning, July 14, 2010.

14. Erik Qualman, *Socialnomics.* Page 51.

15. Heather McBride-Morse, SPHR/GPHR, manager, Human Resources, a Fortune 500 Information Management and Systems company, March 9, 2010.

16. Mike Troiano has spent his early career at top advertising agencies, including McCann-Erickson and Foote, Cone & Belding, and became the founding CEO of Ogilvy & Mather Interactive in 1995. He co-founded New York-based strategic Internet services firm Brandscape in 1996, and merged it with NASDAQ-listed Primix Solutions in late 1998. After the sale of Primix in 2002, he joined venture-funded mobile content pioneer m-Qube, serving as a member of the executive team until the company was bought by VeriSign (Nasdaq: VRSN) in one of the largest Boston-based venture capital exits of 2006. His blog, Scalable Intimacy, is listed on both the AdAge Power150 and Alltop, and he is ranked in the top 1 percent of the most influential people on Twitter. October 8, 2010.

17. Carolyn Rice, April 5, 2010.

18. Lon Safko and David Blake, *The Social Media Bible,* Page 371.

19. Mike Troiano, principal, Holland-Mark, October 8, 2010.

20. Heather McBride-Morse, March 9, 2010.

21. Erik Qualman, interview on December 6, 2010.

22. Lissa Freed, vice president, Human Resources, Activision, August 12, 2010.

23. Carolyn Rice, April 5, 2010.

24. Eric Kaulfuss, director, Talent, CIGNA, August 17, 2010.
25. Heather Huhman, "How to Develop and Maintain Your Personal Brand on Twitter." Retrieved October 12, 2010: *http://www. personalbrandingblog.com/how-to-develop-and-maintain-your-personal-brand-on-twitter/.*
26. Erik Qualman, December 6, 2010.
27. Laura Terenzi Khaleel, September 10, 2010.
28. Mike Troiano, October 8, 2010.

Chapter 2

🔖 *Pull-out Quotation:* Laurie Byrne, vice president, Global Staffing and Talent Development, Stryker Corporation, September 7, 2010.
1. Daniel H. Pink, *Drive, The Surprising Truth About What Motivates Us,* Books on Tape, 2009.
2. Rodney Smith, *Stepping Out of Self-Deception.* Page 143.
3. Matt Lavery, August 3, 2010.
4. Dan McMackin, manager, Public Relations, UPS, August 3, 2010.
5. Lisa Beauclaire, specialist, Human Resources, Sourcing and Diversity, American Family Insurance, September 16, 2010.
6. Cindy Nicola, vice president, Global Talent Acquisition, Electronic Arts, October 6, 2010.
7. Brian Jensen, vice president, Talent Acquisition, McGraw-Hill, August 9, 2010.
8. Keith McIlvaine, September 22, 2010.
9. Stan Weeks, senior recruiting manager and college relations program manager, Weyerhaeuser, September 1, 2010.
10. Lissa Freed, August 12, 2010.
11. Mike Rickheim, August 30, 2010.
12. Chris Nutile, July 30, 2010.
13. Eric Kaulfuss, August 17, 2010.
14. David McMichael, August 18, 2010.
15. Job posting has been paraphrased from a posting found on Michael Page Int'l, Ref: JSG400003000218741H640210. Retrieved October 15, 2010: *www.jobsdb.com/SG/EN/ Search/Job AdSingleDetail?jobsIdList=400003000218741&sr=1.*

16. Megan Dick, PHR, manager, Human Resources, Cameron, September 14, 2010.

17. Laura Terenzi Khaleel, September 10, 2010.

18. Jim Gattuso, director, Staffing and Recruitment, CSC, August 10, 2010.

19. Kirk Imhof, September 24, 2010.

20. Martin Cepeda, senior university recruiter, Fortune 500 healthcare company, October 8, 2010.

21. Laura Terenzi Khaleel, September 10, 2010.

22. Ian Decker, director, Corporate Recruiting, MetLife, August 17, 2010.

23. Karen Bradbury, assistant vice president, Talent Management Strategies, Unum, August 9, 2010.

24. Chris Nutile, July 30, 2010.

25. Chris Nutile, July 30, 2010.

26. Carolyn Rice, April 5, 2010.

27. Twyla Tharp, *The Creative Habit*. Page 164.

28. Shannon Pelissero, zone manager, Human Resources, PPG, September 27, 2010.

29. Chris Nutile, July 30, 2010.

30. Lissa Freed, August 12, 2010.

31. Paula Cuneo provided the sample resume/Website – *www.wix.com/paulacuneo/resume.*

32. Lisa Beauclaire, September 16, 2010.

33. Stan Weeks, September 1, 2010.

34. Jim Gattuso, August 10, 2010.

35. Shannon Pelissero, September 27, 2010.

36. Lisa Beauclaire, September 16, 2010.

37. Stan Weeks, September 1, 2010.

38. David McMichael, August 18, 2010.

39. Cindy Nicola, October 6, 2010.

40. Vincent Taguiped, manager, Recruitment, Fortune 500 media company, July 29, 2010.

Chapter 3

🌿 *Pull-out Quotation:* Eric E. Kaulfuss, August 17, 2010.
1. Ian Decker, September 1, 2010.
2. Brian Jensen, August 9, 2010.
3. Laurie Byrne, September 7, 2010.
4. Mike Rickheim, September 24, 2010.
5. Definition of "six degrees of separation." Retrieved on May 2, 2010: *http://en.wikipedia.org/wiki/Six_degrees_of_separation.*
6. David McMichael, August 18, 2010.
7. Karen Bradbury, August 9, 2010.
8. Mike Rickheim, September 24, 2010.
9. Laura Terenzi Khaleel, September 10, 2010.
10. Abigail Whiffen, director, Global Recruiting Operations, Unisys, September 22, 2010.
11. Eric Kaulfuss, August 17, 2010.
12. Definition of a social network. Retrieved on June 1, 2010: *http://en.wikipedia.org/wiki/ Social_network.*
13. Martin Cepeda, October 8, 2010.
14. Charlotte Frank, PhD, senior vice president, Research and Development, McGraw-Hill, July 21, 2010.
15. Lissa Freed, August 12, 2010.
16. Ian Decker, September 1, 2010.
17. LinkedIn "About Us." Retrieved October 25, 2010: *http://press.linkedin.com/.*
18. Lisa Whittington, vice president, Human Resources, Host Hotels & Resorts, March 10, 2010.
19. Ron Gosdeck, vice president, Recruitment, Unisys, September 22, 2010.
20. Claudia Reilly, July 29, 2010.
21. Jim Gattuso, August 10, 2010.
22. Kathy Hooson, recruiter, Staffing, Hewlett-Packard, November 8, 2010.
23. Kirk Imhof, September 24, 2010.
24. Claudia Reilly, July 29, 2010.

25. Chris Nutile, July 30, 2010.
26. Laura Terenzi Khaleel, September 10, 2010.
27. Carolyn Rice, April 5, 2010.
28. Paul Marchand, vice president, Global Talent Acquisition, PepsiCo, October 27, 2010.
29. Eric Kaulfuss, August 17, 2010.
30. Shally Steckerl, executive vice president, Arbita, August 19, 2010.

Chapter 4

(𝕔) *Pull-out Quotation:* Cindy Nicola, October 6, 2010.
1. Chris Nutile, July 30, 2010.
2. Jeff Rosen, "The Web Means the End of Forgetting," *New YorkTimes,* July 19,2010.
3. Ron Sylvester, "Work key to long life for 102-year-old judge," *Wichita Eagle,* March 1, 2010.
4. *The Business Style Handbook,* Page 42.
5. Claudia Reilly, July 29, 2010.
6. Karen Bradbury, August 9, 2010.
7. Jim Gattuso, August 10, 2010.
8. Matt Lavery, August 3, 2010.
9. Jim Gattuso, August 10, 2010.
10. Dan McMackin, August 3, 2010.
11. Cindy Nicola, October 6, 2010.
12. Jeff Jarvin, *What Would Google Do?* Page 94.
13. Ron Gosdeck, September 22, 2010.
14. Privacy Rights Clearinghouse, Employment Background Checks: A Jobseeker's Guide, Fact Sheet 16: *www.privacy¬rights. org/fs/fs16-bck.htm#2.* See also this *New York Times* article: *www.nytimes.com/2010/12/02/business/smallbusiness/02sbiz. html?src=busln.*
15. Laura Terenzi Khaleel, September 10, 2010.
16. Background checks provide a great deal of information about the prospective employee. Often background checks are not conducted until the final stages of an interview—and they may take

between three to five days—but take a look at the Websites of a few companies that do background checks to get an idea of what's covered. For further information, take a look at USDatalink: *www.usdatalink.com/reports.asp.*

17. Shally Steckerl recommends the following sites to see what kind of information can be revealed in your personal background check: *www.employeescreen.com* or *www.checkster.com.*

Chapter 5

1. Carolyn Rice, April 5, 2010.
2. David McMichael, August 18, 2010.
3. Ian Decker, September 1, 2010.
4. Erik Qualman, Socialnomics, Page XX
5. Vincent Taguiped, July 29, 2010.
6. Jason Fried and David Heinemeier Hansson, *Rework,* Page 193.
7. Erik Qualman was quoting James Carville, "It's the economy, stupid," regarding the statistic about social media being more popular than pornography. Qualman's footnote refers to this Wikipedia entry. Retrieved April 23, 2009: *http://en.wikipedia. org/wiki/It%27s_the_economy,_stupid.*
8. Ian Decker, director, Talent Acquisition, September 1, 2010.
9. Microsoft Study: *http://blogs.technet.com/b/privacyimpera¬tive/ archive/2010/01/27/microsoft-releases-a-study-on-data-privacy-day.aspx.*
10. Laurie Byrne, September 7, 2010.
11. Carolyn Rice, April 5, 2010.
12. Scott Taylor, partner, McDonalds, November 6, 2010.
13. Mike Rickheim, August 30, 2010.
14. Lisa Whittington, March 10, 2010.
15. David McMichael, August 18, 2010.
16. Martin Cepeda, October 8, 2010.
17. Ian Decker, MetLife, September 1, 2010.
18. Matt Lavery, August 3, 2010.
19. Mike Rickheim, August 30, 2010.

20. Jason Fried and David Heinemeier Hansson, *Rework,* Page 231.

Chapter 6

☥ *Pull-out Quotation:* David McMichael, August 18, 2010.
1. Mike Troiano, October 8, 2010.
2. Abigail Whiffen, September 22, 2010.
3. Shally Steckerl, August 19, 2010.
4. Shelley Bird, executive vice president, Public Affairs, Cardinal Health, January 30, 2007.
5. Chris Nutile, July 30, 2010.
6. David McMichael, August 18, 2010.
7. Christ Nutile, July 30, 2010.
8. Laurie Byrne, September 7, 2010.
9. Karen Bradbury, August 9, 2010.
10. Shally Steckerl, August 19, 2010.
11. Matt Lavery, August 3, 2010.
12. Shally Steckerl, August 19, 2010.
13. Laura Terenzi Khaleel, September 10, 2010.
14. Fareed Zakaria, "How to Restore the American Dream," *Time,* October 1, 2010. Retrieved October 22, 2010: *www. time.com/ time/nation/article/0,8599,2026776,00.html.*
15. Mike Troiano, October 8, 2010.
16. Laurie Byrne, September 7, 2010.
17. Mike Troiano, October 8, 2010.
18. Steve Shapiro link, via tweet by Peter Winick on Twitter, October 10, 2010. *http://thoughtleadershipleverage.com/2010/10/ steve-shapiro-personality-poker-why-the-person-you-like-the-least-is-the-person-you-need-the-most/.*
19. Ken Nussbaum, CPA/PFS, JD, K. Nussbaum & Associates, August 12, 2010.
20. Chris Nutile, July 30, 2010.

Chapter 7

🌍 *Pull-out Quotation*: Kirk Imhof, September 24, 2010.

1. Brett Goodman, July 14, 2010.
2. Lissa Freed, August 12, 2010.
3. Paul Marchand, October 27, 2010.
4. Ron Gosdeck, September 22, 2010.
5. Paul Marchand, October 27, 2010.
6. Michael Peltyn, vice president, Human Resources, ARIA-City Center, MGM Resorts International, August 17, 2010.
7. Lisa Beauclaire, September 16, 2010.
8. Brian Jensen, August 9, 2010.
9. Cindy Nicola, October 6, 2010.
10. Martin Cepeda, October 8, 2010.
11. Sean Splaine, leadership recruiter, Google, October 15, 2010.
12. Claudia Reilly, national program manager, Recruitment, July 29, 2010.
13. Jason Fried and David Heinemeier Hansson, *Rework*. Page 210.
14. Claudia Reilly, July 29, 2010.
15. Lissa Freed, August 12, 2010.
16. Debbie Mathew, strategic business partner, Human Resources, Hewlett-Packard, July 28, 2010.
17. Stan Weeks, September 1, 2010.
18. Vincent Taguiped, July 29, 2010.
19. Brett Goodman, July 14, 2010.
20. Daniel H. Pink, Drive, Books on Tape, 2009.

Chapter 8

🌍 *Pull-out Quotation:* Matt Lavery, August 3, 2010.

1. Vincent Taguiped, July 29, 2010.
2. Boolean logic forms the basis of digital electronics. George Boole, a self-educated, Irish mathematician, used an algebraic system to discover logical relationships (using or, and, not) when he was a professor at University College, Cork (Ireland) in 1855.

3. David McMichael, August 18, 2010.
4. Mike Rickheim, August 30, 2010.
5. Ken Nussbaum, August 12, 2010.
6. Laura Terenzi Khaleel, September 10, 2010.
7. Jim Gattuso, August 10, 2010.
8. Shally Steckerl, August 19, 2010.
9. Cindy Nicola, "Engagement, the Candidate Journey, and Social Media: the EA Story," *Journal of Corporate Recruiting Leadership,* May 2010.
10. Lisa Beauclaire, September 16, 2010.
11. Lady Gaga: "It is a promising morning when your eyelash falls in your Folgers." *http://twitpic.com/3935tz.*
12. Laura Terenzi Khaleel, September 10, 2010.
13. Sign up for TweetMyJOBS at *https://tweetmyjobs.com/users/new* to get a Personal Branding Guide. For an update on the numbers of people using Twitter, see **http://gorumors.com/ crunchies/ twitter-monthly-growth-rate/.*
14. Laura Terenzi Khaleel, September 10, 2010.
15. David McMichael, SAIC, August 18, 2010.
16. Chris Nutile, July 30, 2010.
17. Claudia Reilly, July 29, 2010.
18. Chris Nutile, July 30, 2010.
19. Vincent Taguiped, July 29, 2010.
20. Matt Lavery, August 3, 2010.
21. Paul Marchand, October 27, 2010.
22. Paul Marchand, October 27, 2010.
23. Mike Rickheim, August 30, 2010.
24. Chris Nutile, July 30, 2010.
25. Shelley Bird, January 30, 2007.
26. Laura Terenzi Khaleel, September 10, 2010.
27. Kirk Imhof, September 24, 2010.
28. Shannon Pelissero, September 27, 2010.
29. Fareed Zakaria, "How to Restore the American Dream," *Time,* October 1, 2010, Retrieved October 22, 2010: *www. time.com/ time/nation/article/0,8599,2026776,00.html.*
30. Mike Troiano, October 8, 2010.

Chapter 9

🌐 *Pull-out Quotation:* Kirk Imhof, September 24, 2010.

1. Shannon Pelissero, September 27, 2010.
2. Shelley Bird, January 30, 2007.
3. Paul Marchand, October 27, 2010.
4. Jim Gattuso, August 10, 2010.
5. Lisa Beauclaire, September 16, 2010.
6. Keith McIlvaine, September 22, 2010.
7. Shannon Pelissero, September 27, 2010.
8. Paul Marchand, October 27, 2010.
9. Sean Splaine, October 15, 2010.
10. Laura Terenzi Khaleel, September 10, 2010.
11. Eric Kaulfuss, August 17, 2010.
12. Erik Qualman, December 6, 2010.
13. Martin Cepeda, October 8, 2010.
14. Megan Dick, September 14, 2010.
15. Rebecca Shafir, *The Zen of Listening,* Page 215.
16. Kathy Hooson, November 8, 2010.
17. Ian Decker, September 1, 2010.
18. Dan McMackin, August 3, 2010.
19. Stan Weeks, September 1, 2010.
20. Carolyn Rice, April 5, 2010.
21. Eric Kaulfuss, August 17, 2010.
22. Lissa Freed, August 12, 2010.
23. Michael Peltyn, August 17, 2010.
24. Eric Kaulfuss, August 17, 2010.
25. Brett Goodman, July 14, 2010.
26. Paul Marchand, October 27, 2010.
27. Shannon Pelissero, September 27, 2010.
28. Paul Marchand, October 27, 2010.

Chapter 10
ⓨ *Pull-out Quotation:* Shally Steckerl, August 19, 2010.
1. Jim Gattuso, August 10, 2010.
2. Eric Kaulfuss, August 17, 2010.
3. Cindy Nicola, "Engagement, the Candidate Journey, and Social Media: the EA Story," *Journal of Corporate Recruiting Leadership,* May 2010.
4. Cindy Nicola, October 6, 2010.
5. Mike Rickheim, August 30, 2010.
6. Mike Rickheim, August 30, 2010.
7. Shally Steckerl, August 19, 2010.
8. Larry Weber, *Marketing to the Social Web,* Page 215.
9. Marshall McLuhan, *Understanding: The Extensions of Man,* Page 58.
10. Carolyn Rice, April 5, 2010.
11. Kermit Patteson, "How to Market Your Business with Facebook," *New York Times,* November 11, 2009.
12. Lisa Beauclaire, September 16, 2010.
13. Kirk Imhof, September 24, 2010.
14. Debra Black, "Oil spill 'Jersey Shore,' Palin inspire top words of 2010," Retrieved December 5, 2010: *www.thestar.com/printarticle/891056.*
15. Douglas MacMillan, *Bloomberg Businessweek,* June 10, 2010. Retrieved December 3, 2010: *www.businessweek.com/technology/content/jun2010/ tc2010061_650057.htm.*
16. Lissa Freed, August 12, 2010.
17. Heather McBride-Morse, March 9, 2010.
18. Laura Terenzi Khaleel, September 10, 2010.
19. Shannon Pelissero, September 27, 2010.
20. Lisa Beauclaire, September 16, 2010.
21. Laurie Byrne, September 7, 2010.
22. James Suroweicki, *The Wisdom of Crowds,* Page 276.

23. Matt Richtel, "Growing Up Digital – Wired for Distraction," *New York Times,* November 21, 2010. Retrieved November 23: *www.nytimes. com/2010/11/21/technology/21brain.html.*

24. Scott Patterson, *The Quants, How a New Breed of Math Whizzes Conquered Wall Street and Nearly Destroyed It,* read by Mike Chamberlain, Random House Audio Book.

25. Chris Anderson, Talk on "Ted Ideas Worth Spreading." Retrieved November 11, 2010: *www.ted.com/talks/lang/eng/ chris_anderson_of_wired_on_tech_s_long_tail.html.* See also Amy Pillotin's: "Teaching Design for Change," for shifts in workplace: Retrieved October 31, 2010: *www.ted.com/ talks/emily_pilloton_teaching_design_for_change.html.*

26. James O'Toole, Edward E. Lawler, *The New American Workplace,* Page 222.

27. Ron Gosdeck, September 22, 2010.

28. Michael Peltyn, August 17, 2010.

29. David McMichael, August 18, 2010.

30. Lisa Beauclaire, September 16, 2010.

31. Debbie Mathew, July 28, 2010.

32. Paul Marchand, October 27, 2010.

33. Lisa Beauclaire, September 16, 2010.

34. Shally Steckerl, August 19, 2010.

35. Mike Rickheim, August 30, 2010.

36. Retrieved December 3, 2010: *www.gpsbusinessnews.com/ Nielsen-US-Smartphone-Penetration-to-Be-over-50-in-2011_ a2154.html.*

37. Abigail Whiffen, September 22, 2010.

38. Shally Steckerl, August 19, 2010.

39. Heather McBride-Morse, March 9, 2010.

40. Jim Gattuso, August 10, 2010.

41. David McMichael, August 18, 2010.

42. Barry Libert, Jon Spector (and thousands of other contributors) in *We Are Smarter than Me,* Page 144.

43. Retrieved December 1, 2010: *http://en.wikipedia.org/wiki/Brand_management.*

44. Ron Gosdeck, September 22, 2010.

45. Jim Gattuso, August 10, 2010.

46. Daniel Gardner, *The Science of Fear,* Page 293.

Selected Readings

Besides the interviews we conducted with Fortune 500 hiring professionals and other social media and recruitment insiders, which are detailed in the Acknowledgments and Notes, we relied on the following material for additional information.

Books

Cunningham, Helen, and Brenda Greene. *The Business Style Handbook: An A-to-Z Guide for Writing on the Job with Tips from Communications Experts at the Fortune 500.* New York: McGraw-Hill, 2002.

Fried, Jason, and David Heinemeier Hansson. *Rework.* New York: Crown Business, 2010.

Gardner, Daniel. *The Science of Fear, How the Culture of Fear Manipulates Your Brain.* Penguin Books, London, 2008.

Gladwell, Malcolm. *Outliers: The Story of Success.* Little, New York: Brown and Company, 2008.

Greene, Brenda. *Get the Interview Every Time,* revised and expanded edition, New York: Kaplan Publishing, 2008.

Jarvin, Jeff. *What Would Google Do?* Collins Business, New York, 2009.

Libert, Barry, and Jon Spector and thousands of contributors. *We Are Smarter Than Me.* Upper Saddle River: Wharton School Publishing. Pearson Education, Inc., 2008.

McLuhan, Marshall. *Understanding: The Extensions of Man.* New York: McGraw Hill, 1964.

O'Toole, James, and Edward E. Lawler III. *The New American Workplace.* New York: Palgrave MacMillan, 2006.

Patterson, Scott. *The Quants, How a New Breed of Math Whizzes Conquered Wall Street and Nearly Destroyed It.* Random House Audio Book, 2010.

Pink, Dan H. *Drive: The Surprising Truth about What Motivates Us,* Books on Tape. New York: Random House, 2009.

Qualman, Erik. *Socialnomics.* Hoboken, N.J.: John Wiley & Sons, 2010.

Safko, Lon, and David K. Brake. *The Social Media Bible.* Hoboken, N.J.: John Wiley & Sons, Inc., 2009.

Shafir, Rebecca Z. *The Zen of Listening.* Wheaton, Ill.: Quest Books, 2000.

Smith, Rodney. *Stepping Out of Self-Deception.* Boston: Shambhala Publications, Inc., 2010.

Surowiecki, James. *The Wisdom of Crowds.* New York: Random House, 2005.

Tapscott, Don and Anthony D. Williams. *Wikinomics, How Mass Collaboration Changes Everything.* New York: Penguin Books, 2006.

Tharp, Twyla with Mark Reiter. *The Creative Habit.* New York: Simon & Schuster, 2003.

Tracy, Brian. *Eat That Frog,* Audiobook. BBC Audiobooks America; Unabridged edition, November 8, 2006.

Articles

Definition of "six degrees of separation." Retrieved May 2, 2010. *http://en.wikipedia.org/wiki/Six_degrees_of_separation.*

Definition of a social network: Retrieved June 1, 2010. *http://en.wikipedia.org/wiki/Social_network.*

Huhman, Heather, "How to Develop and Maintain Your Personal Brand on Twitter." Retrieved October 12, 2010. *www.personalbrandingblog.com/how-to-develop-and-maintain-your-personal-brand-on-twitter/.*

Internet World Users by Language: Top 10 Languages, June 30, 2010. Retrieved September 22, 2010. *www.internetworldstats.com/stats7.htm.*

Jenkins, Holman, "Google and the Search for the Future," *Wall Street Journal,* August 14, 2010. Retrieved September 10, 2010. *http://online.wsj.com/article/SB10001424052748704901104575423294099527212.html*

LinkedIn, About Us: Retrieved October 25, 2010. *http://press.linkedin.com/.*

MacMillan, Douglas, *Bloomberg Businessweek,* June 10, 2010. *www.businessweek.com/technology/content/jun2010 tc2010061_650057.htm. Retrieved December 3, 2010.*

Michael Page International, Ref: JSG400003000218741H640210. Retrieved October 15, 2010. *www.jobsdb.com/SG/EN/Search/JobAdSingleDetail?jobsIdList=400003000218741&sr=1.*

Needleman, Sarah, "Internal Hires, Referrals Were Most Hired in 2009," *WSJ* online. February 25, 2010. Retrieved October 1, 2010. *http://online.wsj.com/article/SB100014240527487033150045750737504228898806.html.*

Nicola, Cindy, "Engagement, the Candidate Journey, and Social Media: the EA Story," *Journal of Corporate Recruiting Leadership,* May 2010.

O'Reilly, Tim, "What Is Web 2.0: Design Patterns and Business Models for the Next Generation of Software," *http://oreilly.com/web2/archive/what-is-web-20.html*.

Patteson, Kermit, "How to Market Your Business with Facebook," *New York Times*, November 11, 2009.

Richtel, Matt, "Growing Up Digital – Wired for Distraction," *New York Times*, November 21, 2010. *www.nytimes.com/2010/11/21/technology/21brain.html*.

Rosen, Jeffrey, "The Web Means the End of Forgetting," *New York Times*, July 19, 2010.

Rugaber, Christopher S. *Associated Press.* "Economy loses 95K jobs due to government layoffs," Retrieved October 8, 2010. *http://politics.usnews.com/news/articles/2010/10/08/economy-loses-95k-jobs-due-to-government-layoffs.html*.

"Starbucks Most Popular Brand on Social Networking Sites," Retrieved October 8, 2010. *http://techie-buzz.com/social-networking/starbucks-most-popular-brand-on-social-networking-sites.html*

Steel, Emily and Geoffrey A. Fowler, "Facebook in Privacy Breach," WSJ.com. Retrieved October 18, 2010. *http://online.wsj.com/article/SB10001424052702304772804575558484075236968.html*

Sutter, John D, CNN "English gets millionth word on Wednesday, site says," Retrieved October 2, 2010. *http://articles.cnn.com/2009-06-10/tech/million.words_1_global-language-monitor-millionth-word-new-words?_s=PM:TECH*.

Sylvester, Ron, "Work key to long life for 102-year-old judge," *Wichita Eagle*, March 1, 2010. Retrieved June 20, 2010. *www.kansas.com/2010/03/01/1204128/work-key-to-long-life-for-102.html*.

Wolgemuth, Liz, "What the Resumes of Top CEOs Have in Common," *U.S. News & World Report*, May 21, 2010. Retrieved May 24, 2010. *http://finance.yahoo.com/news/What-the-Resumes-of-Top-CEOs-usnews-1845675616.html?x=0*.

Zakaria, Fareed, "How to Restore the American Dream," Time, October 21, 2010. Retrieved November 1, 2010. *www.time.com/time/nation/article/0,8599,2026776,00.html*.

Videos

Emily Pilloton, Ted Ideas Worth Spreading
www.ted.com/talks/emily_pilloton_teaching_design_for_change.
html.

Chris Anderson, Ted Ideas Worth Spreading
*www.ted.com/talks/lang/eng/chris_anderson_of_wired_on_*
tech_s_long_tail.html.

Index

blogs, 36, 40, 45, 122, 140, 144, 182
Boolean logic, 139
bots, 87
Bradbury, Karen, 55, 74, 94, 120
brand management, the principles
　　of, 185
brand yourself, 111
brand,
　　build your personal, 99
　　leveraging your personal, 167
　　your personal, 105, 132, 153,
　　　　168-169, 185
branding, 143
　　personal, 17, 25-42
Brass Ring, 64
build a brand, 175
business cards, 122
Byrne, Coleen, 18-19, 104
Byrne, Laurie, 43, 73, 108, 120,
　　122, 176
Cameron, 51, 158
campus recruitment, 129
Cardinal Health, 118, 150
career
　　fairs, 55, 86, 129, 140, 144,
　　　　152, 162, 183
　　objective, create a, 57
　　site conversion rates, 67
CareerBuilder, 130
Carnegie, Dale, 35
categorize your network, 124
Cepeda, Martin, 53, 78, 110, 132, 156
certification program, 53
certifications, 52
chronological resumes, 59
CIGNA, 39, 49, 71, 77, 85, 155,
　　162-163, 168
classifieds, 142
Classmate.com, 27
CNET, 18, 116-118

cohesive message, send a, 39
communication skills, 65
company
　　culture, 39, 44-45, 131, 153
　　e-mail, 57
compatibility of resumes, 63
competencies, highlight, 33
computer literacy, 145
Computer Science Corporation, 97
contingency recruiter, a, 86
contract work, 160
core competencies, 50
corporate
culture, 161
　　fit, 149
corp-speak, 169
cover letter, the, 68-69, 132-135,
　　145, 155
　　first paragraph of, 69
　　specific, 132
Craigslist, 27, 117-118
creative capital, 64
credentials, 60
credibility, 89
critical listening, 158
CSC, 52, 65, 81, 94, 140, 152,
　　167, 184, 186
cultural fit, 136
Cuneo, Paula, 64
Dahlberg, Tim, 115
Decker, Ian, 21, 55, 72, 80, 105,
　　107, 111, 158
demographics of social networks, 18
develop a brand, 98
Dick, Megan, 51, 158
Digg, 27
digital
　　brand, effective, 108
　　brand, your, 105
discretion, practice, 98

About the Authors

Brenda Greene is a former editor at *Working Woman* magazine and the author of the recently revised *Get the Interview Every Time: Proven Resume and Cover Letter Strategies from Fortune 500 Hiring Professionals.* She coauthored *The Business Style Handbook* and *America's Girl,* a biography of Gertrude Ederle, the first woman to swim the English Channel. It recently won the International Swimming Hall of Fame Buck Dawson award. Brenda recently moved to Enfield, North Carolina.

First-time author **Coleen Byrne** has more than 14 years of experience working in the Internet industry. She has both international and domestic experience working in Internet Advertising Sales and Operations, Marketing, and Business Development. She has worked for giants of the World Wide Web such as: Excite@Home, CNET: The Computer Network (a division of CBS Interactive), and IGN Entertainment (a division of News Corp). Most recently, Coleen was the Southwest Sales Director for Yahoo! With her work inextricably connected to the Internet almost from its inception, Coleen's career network and relationships have always been linked to social networking. Coleen currently resides in the Seattle area with her husband, Ryan, and two sons, Myles and Liam.

15.99